Elegant ELK

Delicious DEER

ELEGANT ELK - DELICIOUS DEER

First Edition, 1978

Third Printing, 1985

Copyright © 1978 by JUDY BARBOUR, Bay City, Texas
Published by PAUL PETERS STUDIO, Palacios, Texas

Library of Congress Catalog Number 78-50099
ISBN 0-686-33178-8

Design and Typography by Paul Peters Studio, Palacios, Texas
Photograph of Grand Tetons by Barry Barbour, Bay City, Texas
Photograph of Author by Paul Peters Studio, Palacios, Texas
Line Illustrations by Cindy Garetson, Jackson, Wyoming
Printed in the United States of America by Publishers Press, Salt Lake City, Utah

This volume is Dedicated with Love to.....

MY HUSBAND, BARRY, THE HUNTER
(Who taught me how to cook!)

and to.....

MY BOYS, DONALD AND BARRY
(Who love to hunt as well as to eat)

Judy Barbour

ELEGANT ELK - DELICIOUS DEER

So your husband the hunter, has bagged his big game - a magnificent Elk or Deer. Now, what are you going to do with it?

For years my husband went hunting. For years he brought home the game. For years we packed it in our freezer; and eventually, gave most of it away. The remainder was generally prepared as Swiss Steak, as that was the only way I could prepare wild game well. We certainly did tire of Swiss Steak!

Then as a revelation, I faced a challenge - to see what I could do with the wild game that was different and exciting; something I would be proud to serve for an elegant dinner. This book is the product of that challenge!

Now, I can honestly say that my family actually prefers the wild game to other meats. It is not as fat, has a very small amount of cholesterol, no stilbestrol and consequently, is much better nutritionally for you.

THIS BOOK IS FOR YOU, THE HUNTER'S WIFE. Lucky you! I have searched the bookshelves for such a publication and was unable to find many imaginative recipes for wild game. So as a result, I wrote my own. I have concentrated my recipes mostly on the preparation of Elk and Deer as these are the most popular game animals bagged by most hunters. I have also included some unusual recipes for the preparation of other game, as well as some game bird recipes.

I have received much encouragement to write this cookbook. It not only contains many fantastic wild game recipes, but also many exciting accompaniments as well.

HAVE FUN!

Judy

I'M JUDY . . . .

I'M THE HUNTER'S WIFE . . . . . and the mother of two boys who also enjoy hunting.
I'M A PROFESSIONAL MODEL . . . . . trained at Houston's most prestigious studios.
I'M A COMMERCIAL PILOT . . . . . with both single and multi-engine ratings; and plan
to become a certified ground-school instructor.
BARRY, MY HUSBAND, and I are both pilots of our own twin-engine Cessna 310.
I'M AN ELEMENTARY EDUCATION MAJOR . . . . . of the University of Houston.
I'M A PAST-PRESIDENT . . . . . of the Junior Service League of Bay City, Texas.
I'M A MEMBER . . . . . of the First Presbyterian Church of Bay City, Texas.

I MOST ENJOY BEING A HOMEMAKER . . . . . and I love to cook! But I especially do love flying,
modeling and trap-shooting - and I enjoy studying
and collecting fine jewelery.

Both my husband and I are native Texans. Barry is a noted big-game hunter, having hunted exten-
sively in the North American continent for many years. He has a fantastic collection of trophies!
He and his partner own a hunting outfit - FLEMING & BARBOUR Big Game Outfitters, in Jackson,
Wyoming; where we now reside for four and a half months of each year.

IT IS BECAUSE OF THE STRONG ASSOCIATION WITH HUNTING THAT I FOUND MYSELF
COMPELLED TO WRITE THIS COOKBOOK.

The Grand Tetons, glorious habitat of the North American Elk and Deer, provided the inspiration for this work of joy. These creatures of the wild regions are as fully majestic in their setting as are the great mountains from whence they come. Throughout history, mankind has hunted for survival as well as sport. The Elk and Deer are two of the most common of the wild game animals. There are many varieties of Deer in our country and practically every state has a legal hunting season on Deer. The Deer multiply rapidly and because of controlled hunting, are not allowed to starve and die from lack of food for the abundant population.

The Elk habitat is limited to the rugged mountain regions of the Northwestern United States. Hunting of the Elk is highly controlled in order to preserve the species. Without controlled hunting, many Elk would die of starvation.

The real hunter and sportsman is a game conservationist. The Elk and Deer are a main food source to many natives of the Elk and Deer producing states. To the hunters that are fortunate enough to bag the game, treasure the meat - as it is indeed a treasure to be able to serve it.

Thus, this is the cookbook with a wide variety of ideas for your preparation of.....
ELEGANT ELK - DELICIOUS DEER!

RETAIL CUTS OF ELK AND DEER

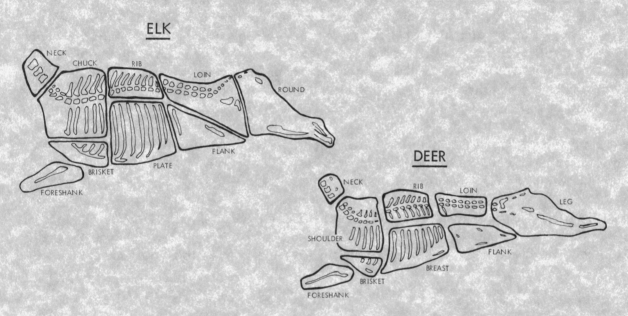

ELK

NECK
CHUCK
RIB
LOIN
ROUND
FLANK
BRISKET
PLATE
FORESHANK

DEER

NECK
RIB
LOIN
LEG
SHOULDER
FLANK
BREAST
BRISKET
FORESHANK

Additional Reference: "YOU AND YOUR WILD GAME", Agricultural Extension Service, University of Wyoming, Laramie, Wyoming 82071 (B-613, $1.00)

The manner in which the hunter cares for his game can mean the difference in meat that is delicious and meat which is not fit to serve! To find out exactly how to care for your game, I asked hunting authority Warren Fleming.

Warren is my husband's partner in FLEMING & BARBOUR BIG GAME OUTFITTERS, Jackson, Wyoming. Warren is a third generation native of Jackson and has hunted in the mountains of Northwestern Wyoming all his life. He can tell you the name of practically every mountain and creek, as he has ridden by horseback or walked and hunted them all.

Warren says, "When the animal is killed, if he is not to be caped for a trophy, cut his throat so he will bleed out. After this is done, make an incision under the tail. Cut hide from under the tail to the animal's head.

Using either a saw or axe, cut the pelvis bone. With a knife, cut the lining to where the ribs start. Again, use a saw or axe to cut the brisket. Then using a knife, cut the diaphragm on both sides to the backbone. Hold the windpipe, and make two incisions in the windpipe for index finger and middle finger, and pull out all the entrails. At the same time, cut entrails loose from the animal's back. By this time, the entrails should be completely out of the animal.

Remove the head with a saw or axe, making sure the windpipe is completely removed from the carcass, because this is where spoiling of the meat can start. If animal is to be left overnight, cut legs at the knee joints with an axe. Split backbone carefully, so as not to cut the hide. This assures that the shoulders will cool out. When finished, the carcass should be lying open, resembling a basket.

Cover the animal with pine boughs to keep the birds away. If the animal is to be packed by horse, quarter him in four pieces leaving two ribs on each hindquarter. If the weather is hot, take to cold storage immediately. Age at least ten days before cutting meat."

TABLE OF CONTENTS

IMAGINATIVE HAPPENINGS

"For you, a collection of party ideas and menus with flair and imagination. The Wild Game is the main attraction.

You may use the Wild Game for an elegant party, not just something you serve your family when the food budget is low.

Because you do not have to purchase expensive meat, you may splurge on other things such as fresh caviar and fresh flowers."

LET'S CELEBRATE! DINNER PARTY

Champagne Tony   Wyoming Wapiti
Stuffed Mushrooms   Tossed Salad with Condiments
Stuffed Artichokes   Snow King Treats

So you are Judy the Wife, Judy the Mother, Judy the Daughter, Judy the Chauffeur, Judy the Housekeeper, and Judy the Volunteer. The list goes on and on!

You have finally found the time to be just JUDY – and do something you have always wanted to do. You just got your multi-engine rating from mountain-flying authority and FAA Examiner, Sparky Imeson; flying in the majestic, rugged Teton Mountain country. You're still flying high!

This calls for a celebration! You invite a few special friends over to share your joy. The menu is rather time-consuming to prepare, but worth your time and effort for such an exciting occasion. Of course, you will want to set an elegant table with fresh flowers, silver, crystal, china, linen napkins and candles. The Sky's the limit!

THE CHRISTMAS COCKTAIL PARTY

Salami Horn of Plenty
Teriyaki Meatballs Fondue
Garlic Cheese Logs
Chips
Crab Mousse
Turkey
Ham
Assorted Breads

Fireside Chili Dip with Corn Chips
Elk and Sausage Pie
Relish Tray
Jalapenos stuffed with Pimiento Cheese
Yummy Brownies
Super Sand Tarts
Champagne Punch with Ice Ring
Coffee

You have been decorating the house for weeks and it is really sparkling. Of course the hunter's trophies are all decked with holly wreaths and red bows around their necks. (Bob Brister, internationally known hunter and outdoor editor, while visiting in our home once during the Christmas holidays, said, "That is how the trophies should look, just as in the woods!"). Everyone is looking forward to your Christmas party, as usual.

Set a beautiful table. Your centerpiece might be a miniature artificial Christmas tree beautifully trimmed with lavish ornaments. Use your Sterling silver candelabra, your silver punchbowl and cups at one end of the serving table, and your silver samovar at the other. Place silver trays and chafing dishes artfully on the table for all the goodies.

PEACE ON EARTH! This is the time to be thankful for family and friends.

HAPPY HUNTING SEND - OFF

Festive Party Punch
Hot Wine
Party Pate' with Assorted Crackers
Elk Shish-Kebab with Rice Pilaf

Zucchini Casserole Amandine
Super Sand Tarts with Sherbet
Coffee

Fall has arrived! Your husband is going hunting. He is really excited, but you just do not share his enthusiasm. You throw a few temper tantrums, and tell him to send your postcards to Las Vegas; but you really know you will be home caring for the children. And don't forget to remind him that the children ALWAYS get sick while he is gone! You know he is going, because he loves to hunt. So you settle down and make the most of it.

Call some good friends and have a Happy Hunting Send-off. Cut out construction paper letters "Happy Hunting" and place on the front entrance door. Fall leaves may be placed in vases throughout the house. A straw cornucopia of fruit and leaves may be the centerpiece. Brass or bronze candelabra would be masculine. Have Fun! Send the hunter off with a smile and a kiss - and go out and buy a new dress!

"ON TARGET" HUNTING WIVES' LUNCHEON

Cold Duck
Avocado Halves stuffed with Caviar
Fresh Fruit Salad in Cantaloupe
Pheasant or Grouse Whiz

Rice
Sourdough French Bread
Southern Pecan Pie

"Hunting Season Has Begun,
Why Don't We Women Have Some Fun?"

This is the way to begin your invitation, cleverly done on target sheets you get at the sporting goods store. Start the party with Cold Duck (not the kind you shoot!). Use leopard print bridge cloths that you make. Also stitch up some zebra print napkins. Center each bridge table with ceramic animals and fresh greenery for a woodsy effect. Browse in the specialty and import shops as well as the variety stores for clever and unique items for decorating tables.

"WE'RE GOING ON A SAFARI" BIRTHDAY PARTY

Birthday Cake

Ice Cream Cones

Fruit Punch

Your young son is turning six and wants to be like Daddy and be a "hunter". Celebrate his special day with a Safari Party.

Invitations are designed by you. Construction paper is perfect with a leopard skin cut from "contact" paper. Excitement begins for the invited guests when each receives his invitation.

Turn the back yard into a jungle with a suspended bridge and grass huts. Cover the party table with a jungle-print sheet. Decorate the cake accordingly. Make up exciting games such as "Pin the Tail on the Lion" or "Drop the Handkerchief Hippo". Dart games are fun, too.

BACK-TO-SCHOOL BASH

A-thru-Z Elk Burgers   Soft Drinks
Assorted Chips   Yummy Brownies

It's late August and time for the children to return to school. Let them invite the gang over for a cookout.

The boys can grill the burgers; the girls can assemble them. All you need is something cool to drink, then Yummy Brownies for dessert. After that, the group can play the stereo and dance.

MEXICAN FIESTA

Nachos
Beer
Sangria
Fireside Chili Dip

South-of-the-Border Salad
Chili Caliente with Rice
Bollos with Jalapeno Jelly
Praline Ice Cream

Mexican Fiestas are such fun!

Use brightly colored table cloths and lots of paper flowers as centerpieces. Hire a Mariachi Band to mingle amongst the guests, or substitute with some fine Mexican music tapes. Let candles predominate. A very informal evening where friends are relaxed and happy. Ole'!

APRES SKI PARTY

Hot Wine
Stuffed Mushrooms
Garlic Cheese Log with Crackers

Rocky Mountain Burgundy Ragout
Crusty French Bread
Bordeaux Wine

After a fantastic day on the slopes, have a get-together to talk it all over.

Have a roaring fire in the fireplace.

Serve the Stuffed Mushrooms and Garlic Cheese Log with the Hot Wine to warm you up. Heat the bread and Rocky Mountain Burgundy Ragout while guests are enjoying the appetizers. Serve the Bordeaux with dinner.

This is a plan-ahead dinner that you prepare the day before. You might even set your table early, so while you are on the slopes you are not preoccupied with your dinner party.

Let it Snow!

HAWAIIAN LUAU

Island Punch
Hawaiian Jerky
Watermelon Basket
Teriyaki Elk or Deer

Fluffy Rice
Honolulu Baked Beans
Coconut Balls

A Luau is a very festive Island celebration.

Create the Island atmosphere by transforming your back yard or patio into a Hawaiian Paradise. Low tables can be made using plywood on bricks. Use flowered cloth for table covers. Place cushions for seating. Use banana leaves, flowers, lanterns and candles to add to the decor. Shells may be used with fruits for the centerpiece. Tiki torches are great. Set out a punch bowl, with real or plastic exotic flowers floating in the punch. Present each guest with a crepe paper Lei upon arrival.

Do the Hula!

CHINESE NEW YEAR

Egg Rolls	Rice
Mimosas	Zucchini Casserole Amandine
Oriental Chicken Soup	Fortune Cookies
Elk Sukiyaki	Saki

Chinese New Year falls in late January or early February, and is the perfect reason for a party when you have the winter "blahs"!

Plan the decorations according to which animal is represented for the New Year. For example, the Year of the Tiger, etc. Design clever invitations. Center the table with a hugh ceramic Tiger, even a fluffy stuffed one! Use Chinese plates if you have them, and chopsticks. The Frozen Egg Rolls will suffice; although you can make your own - easy! Be sure to get Fortune Cookies.

Don't forget confetti and serpentine.

FAMILY GET-TOGETHER BREAKFAST OR BRUNCH

Assorted Juices   Hot Sourdough Biscuits
Milk   Coffee
Wild West Casserole

    The Wild West Casserole, because of the green chilis, has a different taste for a breakfast food. It is an especially nice contrast with the Sourdough Biscuits.

    Your family will love this breakfast!

MOUNTAINSIDE BRUNCH

Mimosas
Elk or Deer Sausage Patties

Fiesta Brunch Eggs
Coffee

Pack a thermos of Mimosas. Take along plastic wine glasses. Serve Mimosas while cooking sausage and omelette.

Spread a red checkered cloth on the mountainside. Use pretty, colorful, coordinated paper plates and napkins. Pick a bouquet of wildflowers or beautiful leaves for a centerpiece. Serve mugs of hot, steaming coffee.

Life is beautiful!

ON THE TRAIL BREAKFAST

Orange Juice   Toast
Elk or Deer Sausage Patties   Hot Coffee
Eggs

This menu is most suitable for a pack-trip or camp-out.

It is simple and uncomplicated - and very hearty.

POSH PICNIC FOR TWO

Indian Summer Sippers
Sausage Quiche
Party Pate with Crackers

Judy's Vegetable Salad
Roast Pheasant or Grouse
Fresh Fruit Pyramid

What could be more romantic than a picnic for two?

Find a really pretty, large straw basket and load it artfully. Spread a cloth on the mountainside. Serve Indian Summer Sippers in goblets. Use candelabra, silver, etc., if you want to go elegant. Let your imagination run wild!

The quiche and pate are for appetizers. Next serve the chilled Roast Pheasant or Grouse and individual servings of the Oriental Vegetable Salad. The fresh fruit pyramid is a beautiful finale to an exciting day!

SPRING BRUNCH ON THE DECK

Jackson Hole Sunrises
Fresh Asparagus Omelette
Sourdough Biscuits

Elk or Deer Sausage Links
Coffee

Mix up a batch of Jackson Hole Sunrises. Serve on the deck as your guests gather.

Center the redwood table with a potted yellow Chrysanthemum, add several ceramic game animals to complement the decor. Sit down at individual places, using lovely animal design plates, or pretty pottery.

Serve the fantastic Omelette, hot homemade Sourdough Biscuits, Sausages, and steaming hot coffee in mugs.

Great way to entertain houseguests!

PARTY BRUNCH

Watermelon Basket filled with Fruits
Miniature Deer or Elk Sausage Patties
Miniature Biscuits
Target Cheese Balls

Cheesy Sausage Balls
Sausage Pinwheels
Champagne Punch
Coffee or Hot Tea

Set a festive table buffet style.

An interesting centerpiece may be a basket of fresh fruits or vegetables, or a beautiful bouquet of flowers. Use your imagination, depending upon the season.

This is a great menu for your committee meeting, ladies' auxiliary, or leisurely couples' brunch on the terrace or at the fireside.

LET'S PACK A LUNCH

Elk Salami   Carrot and Celery Sticks
Pimiento Cheese Sandwiches on Whole Wheat   Back-Pack Energy Snack

So you're going back-packing, hiking or fishing; maybe even bicycling.

You've got to take an energy-packed lunch. This one is good.

Now, you can enjoy the magnificent mountains.

FIRESIDE PARTY

Surprise Balls

Texas Trash

Rendezvous Peak Cave-ins

It's really cold outside! It's snowing heavily.

Start a fire in the fireplace.

Have a party and be cozy!

ITALIAN DINNER BY CANDLELIGHT

Asti Spumonti, chilled
Antipasto Platter
Tossed Salad, Italian Dressing

Italian Spaghetti
Stuffed Artichokes
Espresso Ice

Elk can be elegant by candlelight!

Invite a few friends over. Set the table with an Italian air.....red checkered cloths, candles dripping in wine bottles as holders. Serve chilled Asti Spumonti to add the excitement of a sparkling wine.

Ecco!

ELEGANT EVENING

Champagne Tony
Avocado Halves stuffed with Iranian Caviar
Fresh Spinach Salad with Hot Dressing
Peach Blossom Grouse or Quail

Rice
Fresh Broccoli with Paprika Cheese Sauce
Strawberries Romanoff
Liebfraumilch

You are in the mood to cook!

No special reason or occasion; maybe you just finished your fall housecleaning - and the children are back in school. This allows you some "free" time during the day. Everything is spotless!

Set a beautiful table using the Fall colors for your theme. It is a very unique menu, and one I think your friends will consider very special.

APPEALING APPETIZERS

"Fantastic and intriguing appetizers to accompany your wild game dishes."

ANTIPASTO TRAY

Elk Salami*
Ham
Tuna Chunks
Italian Olives and Peppers

Mixed, washed and chilled raw vegetables:
Cauliflower, Carrots,
Zucchini Strips, Bell Pepper Strips,
Celery Strips

Arrange attractively on a platter and serve as an appetizer.

* I recommend that you have your meat processor make up your Salami. Most are quite experienced; and all that we have had prepared has been excellent. It is a much better approach than experimenting on your own.

CHEESY SAUSAGE BALLS

1 pound Deer Sausage   3/4 pound Cheddar Cheese, grated
3-1/4 cups Biscuit Mix

Combine Cheese and Biscuit Mix, then blend in Deer Sausage, mixing thoroughly and form large ball.
Pinch-off small amounts to roll into balls about 1 inch in diameter.
Bake on a greased cookie sheet at 350 degrees for 12 to 15 minutes.

Great with cocktails or for brunch!

DELICIOUS PIMIENTO CHEESE

2 pounds Velveeta Cheese, grated
3 pounds Rat Trap Cheese, grated
1 quart Mayonnaise
1 large jar Pimientos, grated

1 jar Sweet Relish
1 small can Jalapeno Peppers, chopped
   (or less, to taste)
1/2 teaspoon Garlic Salt
Pinch of Sugar

Mix all ingredients together uniformly.

Serve as a dip or use for a delicious sandwich spread.

FANTASTIC FIRESIDE FONDUE

1/2 cup Catsup
3 tablespoons Prepared Mustard
1/8 cup Oil
2 tablespoons Parsley, minced
Salt and Pepper to taste

2 tablespoons Onion Flakes, minced
2 tablespoons Shallots, chopped
1 teaspoon Worcestershire Sauce
Dash Tabasco Sauce

Blend all ingredients together; to make a really tasty Basic Sauce. Do your own experimentation and come up with some truly interesting variations.

Dip your cooked Meat Cubes in the above sauce or its variations, for an outstanding Fondue.

2 pounds Elk or Deer Tenderloin, cubed, bite-size

Pour about 1-1/2 inches of Peanut Oil into Fondue Pot.
Heat to 400 degrees.
Each person spears Meat Cube on fondue fork or bamboo skewer and cooks Meat in heated oil to suit individual taste.
Dip individual cooked Meat Cubes in the sauce above, or your variation.

CHILI PARTY DIP

1 can Chili, without Beans
  (number two size)
1 pound Cheddar Cheese, grated

2 jars Process Cheese Spread
  (sixteen ounce size)
2 tablespoons Jalapeno Peppers, minced

Combine ingredients in top of double-boiler over low heat.
Stir continuously until Cheese melts and mixture is thoroughly heated.
Pour into chafing-dish to keep warm for serving and to keep soft for dipping.
Serve with Corn Chips or Tortilla Chips.

A spicy party treat!

GARLIC CHEESE LOG

1/2 pound Velveeta Cheese, grated
1/2 pound packaged Pimiento Cheese, grated
1 package (8 ounce size) Cream Cheese

1/2 cup Pecans, chopped
1/4 teaspoon Garlic Powder
Paprika, ground

Allow Cheeses to soften fully at room temperature.
Knead together all Cheeses with hands, blending thoroughly; adding chopped Pecans and Garlic Powder.
Shape into two rolls, forming uniform cylinders, then roll in Paprika to cover outside of rolls.
Wrap in waxed paper and chill to firmness in refrigerator.

Slice and serve circles on saltines or other favorite crackers.
May be stored in refrigerator for about 2 weeks.

CHEESE DOLLARS

1/2 pound Sharp Cheese, grated
1/2 pound Margarine, softened
1 cup Rice Krispies

1 teaspoon Cayenne Pepper
1 teaspoon Salt
2 cups Flour

Mix all ingredients together, blending thoroughly, and form a large ball.
Pinch off marble-sized balls and place on a greased cookie sheet.
Press-out flat, each ball with a fork.
Bake at 350 degrees for 20 minutes.

Delightful; and these freeze well after baking.

FIRESIDE CHILI DIP

1 can (#2 size) Chili with Beans
2 tablespoons Dry Red Wine
1/2 cup Onion, chopped
1/2 cup Green Pepper, chopped

1 jar (1/2 ounce size) Stuffed Olives, sliced
1/8 teaspoon Chili Powder
1 cup Cheddar Cheese, grated

Heat all ingredients together; reserving 1/4 cup Grated Cheese.
Serve in chafing-dish, with reserved Cheese sprinkled on top.
Serve with ample supply of large, dip-size Corn Chips on tray, surrounding chafing-dish.

A real favorite in Texas.

SOMBRERO SNACK DIP

1 pound Elk or Deer, ground
1/2 cup Shallots, chopped
2 cans (eight ounce size) Tomato Sauce
1 Fresh Tomato, peeled and chopped
1 can (fifteen ounces) Kidney Beans

1 to 2 teaspoons Chili Powder
1/2 teaspoon Garlic Salt
2 cups Cheddar Cheese, grated
Tortilla Chips

Brown Meat and Onion.
Add Tomato Sauce, Fresh Tomato, Beans (drained), Chili Powder and Garlic Salt.
Simmer uncovered, over low heat for 20 minutes, stirring occasionally.
Add grated Cheese and stir continuously for 3 or 4 minutes more, to melt and blend-in Cheese.

Serve as a delicious Hot Dip in chafing dish, surrounded by Tortilla Chips.
Serves 4 to 8.

PATE A LA MAISON BARBOUR

2 pounds Elk or Deer Steak
1 Beef Bouillon Cube, crushed
2 pounds Elk or Deer Sausage
1/4 teaspoon Thyme
1 Bay Leaf

2 teaspoons Salt
Freshly Ground Black Pepper
1/4 cup Cognac
Bacon Slices

Remove all fat from the Game Meat. Cut into small pieces and grind in your food processor to paste-like consistency.

Dissolve Bouillon Cube in 1 tablespoon Hot Water and add crumbled Bay Leaf, Salt, Pepper, and Cognac, mixing thoroughly. Blend mixture completely into ground Elk or Deer.

In glass loaf pan (ovenproof), place slices of Bacon on bottom; next, alternating layers of Game Meat mixture and Sausage Meat. Finish with Game Meat mixture and top with additional slices of Bacon.

Cover loaf pan and place in a larger pan of hot water, halfway up the sides. Place this combination on oven rack and bake at 300 degrees for 1 hour or longer, until any fat visible is yellowish in color.

Remove from oven and place baking dish on cooling rack. Place another clean glass loaf pan on top of cooked Meat and weight heavily with anything heavy. (Meat grinder, etc.)

Allow to cool under weight. Then cover Meat with plastic wrap, return top loaf pan only and place in refrigerator to chill thoroughly before serving.

For serving, unmold the Pate on suitable serving plate or tray and cut into thin slices with sharp knife. Serve the thin slices on a variety of crisp crackers as apertifs.

48

TERIYAKI MEATBALLS FONDUE

1 pound Elk or Deer, ground
2 tablespoons Soy Sauce
3 teaspoons Sugar

1/2 teaspoon Onion, grated
Dash Garlic Salt
1/2 cup fine, soft Bread Crumbs

Combine Soy Sauce, Sugar, Onion, Garlic Salt and 1 tablespoon Water. Let stand.
Mix Meat and Bread Crumbs, then stir-in Soy Sauce mixture.
Shape into Meatballs of modest size, suitable for fondue use, and refrigerate until serving time.
Spear individually, on fondue forks or bamboo skewers, and cook in Peanut Oil in fondue pot at
375 degrees, for about 1-1/2 minutes, to taste.
Serve with Barbecue Sauce or Hot Mustard Dip.
Yield; about 5 dozen.

SALAMI HORN OF PLENTY

24 slices Elk Salami, thinly sliced
2 packages (8 ounce size) Cream Cheese
3 tablespoons Fresh Parsley, snipped

3 tablespoons Chives, minced
3 tablespoons Fresh Dill, minced
Salt to taste

Twist each Salami slice into a cornucopia shape, pressing overlapping edges together firmly.
Place in a shallow dish, sealed sides down, cover with foil and chill for several hours.
Whip softened Cream Cheese until smooth and blend in Parsley, Chives and Dill with Salt to taste.
Cover mixture and chill about 1 hour.
With a pastry tube, fill Salami cornucopias with chilled Cheese mixture.
Cover and chill again until ready to serve.

"SURPRISE" BALLS

1 pound Elk, ground
1/2 teaspoon Salt
1/4 teaspoon ground Black Pepper

1 teaspoon Worcestershire Sauce
Dash Tabasco Sauce
1 Garlic Clove, minced

Combine Elk, Salt, Pepper, Worcestershire Sauce, Tabasco Sauce and minced Garlic. Toss gently.
Shape Meat mixture around individual "surprises", forming walnut-sized balls.
Grill or broil for 5 to 10 minutes until they are done to taste.
Yield: 1-1/2 to 2 dozen "Surprises".

Suggestions for "Surprises"

Sweet Pickle Wedges
Stuffed Olives
Ripe, pitted Olives
Cheddar or Swiss Cheese Cubes
Jalapeno Pepper Wedges

Peanuts
Pineapple Tidbits
Sliced Fresh Mushrooms
Anchovy Rolls
Green Pepper Wedges

TARGET CHEESE BALLS

1 jar Bacon-Cheese Spread
3/4 cup Flour
4 tablespoons Butter

Dash Worcestershire Sauce
Dash Tabasco Sauce
Stuffed Olives, drained

Blend together all ingredients, except Olives. Chill.
Shape Cheese mixture around an Olive, forming a ball about 1 inch in diameter.
Bake at 400 degrees for about 12 minutes, or until lightly browned.
Yield: 2-1/2 dozen.

May be frozen, then thawed and baked.

ELEGANT ELK, DELICIOUS DEER
& OTHER GAME MEAT AND BIRDS.

"My wild game entrees have an international flavor; from Italian, Greek, Mexican to Hawaiian, Oriental and Indian and as American as the popular burgers."

MY PERSONAL HINTS FOR SUCCESSFUL PREPARATION OF WILD GAME

First of all, there is a misconception that all Wild Game has a "gamey" taste. Quite the contrary. Wild Game has a distinct flavor which differentiates it from Beef, Lamb, Pork and other meats. Many factors can affect its quality and flavor. Among these are proper handling of the meat, weather conditions affecting diet of the game, time of year the game is killed, and effects of the mating season. Wild Game can well provide some of the most delicious and enticing meat you ever prepared.

While experimenting and tasting, quite frequently I have personally used certain ingredients which enhanced the flavor of Wild Game dishes. For instance, I have found that the addition of Worcestershire Sauce complements the Wild Game meat. In some recipes only a small amount was needed, and in others, a larger amount was helpful. You will also find that I have used Garlic liberally throughout the recipes. Black Pepper is a basic ingredient, used more liberally than with comparative Beef dishes.

Some additional seasonings with which you might experiment when the recipe calls for Beef Bouillon are as follows: Beef Stock, chilled and defatted, from last night's Prime Rib is terrific; always, always save the stock from roasts, steaks chicken, etc., as it is quite nutritious as well as delicious. Bovril is a Beef Extract made in England. It is excellent and may be found in many specialty grocery stores. Kitchen Bouquet and Wyler's Beef Granules are also very good for this purpose.

Wine is another essential ingredient in many of the recipes. I have found that Sherry is quite compatible with Wild Game. As a reminder, cook with Sherry or other wine which is of the quality you would drink. This secret alone can be a factor in the success of a magnificent dish. The use of Beer in some of the recipes creates a special taste which is unequalled!

You will discover that in most instances throughout the book, if a particular recipe calls for Elk, you may substitute Deer or vice-versa.

I hope that you will find my suggestions helpful. As you experiment and adapt my recipes to your personal taste and to that of your family and guests, you will find a true appreciation of the uniqueness of Wild Game dishes.

Only then – will you fully enjoy your adventures with ELEGANT ELK, DELICIOUS DEER!

MY HUSBAND, THE HUNTER'S ABSOLUTELY NOTORIOUS BARBECUE SAUCE

2 Garlic Cloves, chopped
2 Onions, quartered
1 cup Oil
2 cups Vinegar
1-1/2 teaspoons Salt
1 teaspoon Black Pepper

1-1/2 tablespoons Worcestershire Sauce
1 Lemon
2 Jalapeno Peppers, canned
1 teaspoon Powdered Mustard
2 pinches Parsley Flakes

Combine all ingredients in a sauce pan, including the juice of the Lemon and one-half of the squeezed rind.
Place over high heat and bring to a boil, reduce heat and simmer for 30 minutes or until Onions are soft.
If you prefer, a 12 ounce can of Beer may be added to the sauce.
Use sauce to baste any barbecue, baste frequently!

My husband, the hunter, is also a fantastic cook! This is the special sauce he created - and it is great on any meat, whether Steak, Burgers or Birds.

A-THRU-Z ELKBURGERS

Season ground Elk (or Deer) to taste using Garlic Salt, Pepper and Worcestershire Sauce. May be grilled outdoors or broiled in the oven.

ALOHA BURGERS - Cook burgers. Top with Pineapple slice and Maraschino Cherry.

BURGUNDY BURGERS - Baste with Burgundy Wine while cooking.

CHILI BURGERS - Top with heated Chili con Carne, grated Onion and Cheese.

DILL BURGERS - Mix finely-chopped Dill Pickles and seasonings with meat before cooking.

EXOTIC BURGERS - Top burgers with Bean Sprouts, Water Chestnuts and Bamboo Shoots.

FRUIT BURGERS - Top with fresh Grapefruit and Orange sections and grated Coconut.

GREEN PEPPER BURGERS - After cooking, top each burger with a Bell Pepper ring and broil a bit more.

HEALTH BURGERS - Top cooked burgers with Alfalfa Sprouts. Crunchy!

ITALIAN BURGERS - Top with sliced fresh Tomatoes and Mozzarella Cheese. Melt Cheese under broiler.

JAPANESE BURGERS - Baste cooking burgers with Soy Sauce.

KING BURGERS - Two burger patties with sliced Cheddar and Swiss Cheese between.

LEMON-BUTTER BURGERS - Mix Lemon Juice and melter Butter. Use to baste cooking burgers.

MUSHROOM BURGERS - Saute canned Mushrooms in Butter. Use to top cooked burgers.

NACHO BURGERS - Mix meat, seasonings, grated cheese and chopped Jalapenos. Broil. Caliente!

ONION BURGERS - Chop canned, fried Onion Rings and mix with meat. Then cook.

PEANUT BUTTER BURGERS - Top grilled burgers with a dollop of Peanut Butter.

QUICKIE BURGERS - Season meat; grill and eat!

RANCH BURGERS - Top cooked burgers with heated Ranch-Style Beans. Garnish with snipped shallots.

SOUR CREAM BURGERS – Top cooked burgers with dollop of Sour Cream. Sprinkle on snipped Shallots.

TANTALIZING BURGERS – Top cooked burgers with Lettuce, Tomatoes, Olives, Pickle slices, Cheese, Mustard and Mayonnaise.

UNUSUAL BURGERS – Stuff meat with Tomatoes, grated Cheese, Sweet Relish and sliced, stuffed Olives.

VEGETARIAN BURGERS – Cook meat. Top with grated Carrots, Radishes and chopped Celery. Crunch!

WORCESTERSHIRE BURGERS – Baste burgers with Worcestershire Sauce while cooking. Tangy!

X-CITING BURGERS – Season cooked burgers with a spread of Sour Cream and Horseradish to taste. Top with sliced boiled egg and add a spoon of red Caviar. Divine!

YUMMY BURGERS – Grill burgers and top with strips of cooked bacon to eat.

ZUCCHINI BURGERS – Grate fresh Zucchini. Mix with meat and seasonings. Cook. Unusual, nutty taste.

Elk Burgers are the very greatest you can prepare; however, Deer Burgers are good, too. You may think some of these ideas are ridiculous or way out, but I'm just trying to have you use your imagination. Try it; you might like it!

BELL PEPPER RINGS - STUFFED

1-1/2 pounds ground Elk or Deer
1 can Mushrooms
Milk
1/2 cup Bread Crumbs
3 tablespoons Onion, grated
1 teaspoon Worcestershire Sauce

1-1/2 teaspoon Salt
1/4 teaspoon Pepper
1 Egg, beaten
2 large Green Peppers
3 tablespoons Catsup
1/2 to 1 cup Cheddar Cheese

Drain Mushrooms, reserving liquid. Add Milk to Mushroom Liquid to make total of 1/2 cup liquid.
Combine Meat, Mushrooms (sliced), 1/2 cup liquid, Bread Crumbs, Onion, Worcestershire Sauce,
Salt, Pepper and Egg (beaten).
Remove ends and seeds from Peppers. Cut into three 1 inch rings. Place Green Peppers in a shallow
baking dish and pack Meat mixture into Pepper rings.
Bake at 350 degrees for 35 minutes. Combine Catsup and Grated Cheese; and spoon over patties.
Continue baking for additional 10 minutes.
Serves 4.

BLACK BEAR ROAST

3 to 4 pound roast of Black Bear
Salt and Pepper
3 Garlic Cloves

Bacon
3 Onions, quartered
2 teaspoons Beef Extract

Make slivers in the roast and insert pieces of the Garlic Cloves, enabling the flavor to penetrate the meat. Salt and Pepper to taste.
Place in roasting pan and place Bacon slices across the top of the meat.
Add quartered Onions, Beef Extract and 2 cups Water.
Roast uncovered at 325 degrees until tender.
Serves 6 to 8.

BAKED QUAIL

Eight Quail
Italian Salad Dressing

Salt and Pepper
One Garlic Clove

Place Dressed Quail in large piece of heavy-duty foil.

Salt and Pepper to taste. Add 1 Garlic Clove and 1 cup Italian Salad Dressing. Fold foil together securely.

Bake at 350 degrees for 1 hour, shaking occasionally.

This makes for tender, juicy birds.

BARBECUED DEER RIBS

Three pounds Deer Ribs.
Barbecue Sauce:

3/4 cup Molasses
3/4 cup Catsup
1 Onion, chopped
2 Garlic Cloves, minced
1/2 teaspoon Salt
1/4 teaspoon Pepper
Dash Tabasco Sauce

Dash Worcestershire Sauce
1/3 cup Orange Juice
3 or 4 Whole Cloves
2 tablespoons Oil
2 tablespoons Vinegar
1 teaspoon Prepared Mustard

Arrange meat on shallow roasting pan. Cover with foil. Bake 30 minutes in 325 degree oven. Pour off excess fat if any, and bake 30 minutes longer.
Combine all ingredients for Barbecue Sauce. Bring to boil, reduce heat and simmer 5 minutes. Pour Sauce over Ribs. Bake at 400 degrees uncovered, basting often, for 45 minutes or until tender and browned.
Serves 4 to 6.

BROILED QUAIL OR DOVES - SOUTH TEXAS STYLE

Eight Quail or Doves
4 Jalapeno Peppers, canned

Salt and Pepper
8 Bacon slices

Salt and Pepper Quail or Doves.
Split canned Jalapenos lengthwise and insert in cavity of each bird. (Keep fingers away from eyes).
Wrap one slice of Bacon around each bird and secure with round toothpick.
Broil in oven breast side up. Turn and cook to desired brownness.
Place on lower rack and bake at 350 degrees about 45 minutes, or until tender.
May also be grilled.
Serves 1 hunter or 4 guests.

CANTONESE ELK AND SNOW PEAS

1 pound Elk Steak, sliced with the grain
1-1/2 teaspoon Cornstarch
Peanut Oil

2 pounds fresh Chinese Snow Peas
2 tablespoons Soy Sauce
Salt and Pepper

Mix Elk meat, Cornstarch and 2 teaspoons of Peanut Oil.
Stir-fry meat in oil in a Chinese Wok over high heat until it loses its red color. Set aside meat.
Heat 2 tablespoons oil and stir-fry Snow Peas one minute, until they turn a brilliant green.
Do not overcook!
Return meat to wok, season with additional Soy Sauce, Salt and Pepper.
Serve with rice.
Serves 4 to 6.

CHILES RELLENOS ELK

1 pound Ground Elk or Deer
1/2 cup Chopped Onion
2 four ounce cans Green Chiles, drained
8 ounces Shredded Cheddar Cheese
1-1/2 cups Milk

4 Eggs, beaten
1/4 cup Flour
1/2 teaspoon Salt
1/2 teaspoon Hot Pepper Sauce
1/8 teaspoon Pepper

Brown Ground Meat and Onion. Sprinkle with Salt and Pepper.
Halve Chiles crosswise and remove seeds.
Place half the Chiles in a 2 quart baking dish. Sprinkle with half of shredded Cheese. Top with Meat mixture and arrange remaining Chiles over Meat.
Combine remaining ingredients, beating until smooth. Pour over Chiles.
Bake at 350 degrees for 45 minutes.
Top with remaining Cheese and cook 5 to 10 minutes more. Cool 5 minutes.
Serves 6.

CHILI CON CARNE

4 pounds Ground Elk or Deer
3 Garlic Cloves, minced
2 tablespoons Oil
4 large Bell Peppers, slivered
6 large Onions, chopped
3 one pound cans Tomatoes
4 one pound cans Kidney Beans, drained

2 six ounce cans Tomato Paste
1/4 cup Chili Powder
2 teaspoons White Vinegar
1/4 teaspoon Red Cayenne Pepper
3 whole Cloves
1 Bay Leaf
Salt and Pepper

Cook Garlic in Oil until golden. Then add Meat and brown.
Add Onions and Bell Peppers. Add balance of ingredients, with Salt and Pepper to taste.
Cover and cook slowly for 1 hour. If too dry, add additional Tomatoes.
Serve with Rice and Crackers.
Great on a cold night!
Serves 8 to 10.

CHILI CALIENTE!

2 pounds cubed Elk or Deer
1 teaspoon Oregano
1 teaspoon Cumin
4 teaspoons Chili Powder
2 cloves Garlic, minced

1 small can Pimiento, chopped
2 tablespoons Oil
1/2 teaspoon Cayenne Pepper
1 tablespoon Flour
1 one pound can Kidney Beans

Cube Meat. Brown in Oil. Add 2 cups Water.
Add Oregano, Cumin, Chili Powder, Garlic, Pimiento and Pepper.
Bring to a boil; then simmer for 2-1/2 hours.
Stir in Flour to thicken, add Beans and simmer for 20 minutes more.

Serve with Tortillas, Rice, Tossed Salad and a pitcher of Beer.
Fresh Fruit and Coffee for dessert.
Ole!

ELKBURGER PIZZA

2-1/2 pounds ground Elk
1/2 cup Bread Crumbs
1 Onion, chopped
1 teaspoon Salt
1/4 teaspoon Pepper
1/2 cup Milk
1 can Tomato Sauce
1 Garlic Clove, minced

1 cup Romano Cheese, grated
Pepperoni slices
Fresh Mushrooms, sliced
1 can Anchovy Fillets
1 cup Ripe Olives, sliced
1 cup Stuffed Olives, sliced
Mozzarella Cheese, shredded

Combine Meat, Bread Crumbs, Onion, Salt, Pepper and Milk. Mix lightly and pat into 14 inch Pizza Pan.
Mix Tomato Sauce and minced Garlic. Spread over Meat Mixture. Top with grated Romano Cheese.
Arrange Pepperoni, Mushrooms, Anchovies and Olives on top. Sprinkle with Mozzarella Cheese.
Bake at 450 degrees for 20 to 30 minutes.
Cut into wedges.
Serves 6 to 8.

TENDERLOIN ROTEL

4 to 5 pounds Elk or Deer Tenderloin   1 can Rotel Tomatoes with Green Chiles
3 to 4 tablespoons Oil   Salt and Pepper to taste.

Slice the Tenderloin across the grain into slices about 1/8 to 1/4 inch thick.
Brown in skillet in oil, until Oil is absorbed.
Chop canned Tomatoes quite fine and add Tomatoes and Juice to skillet, cooking
meat until most of the juice is absorbed.
Salt and Pepper to taste.

This makes a great appetizer, or use as an entree.

THE BOYS' FAVORITE ELK OR DEER

4 to 6 pounds Elk or Deer Steak
2 tablespoons Oil

1/4 to 1/2 cup Soy Sauce
Black Pepper

Cut Steak into finger-size strips.
Brown in a heavy skillet in Oil, stirring to prevent sticking.
Add Soy Sauce and Black Pepper to taste. Cover and simmer about ten minutes.
Excellent, served with Hot Rice.
This serves 3 or 4 hungry boys!
Sometimes, I serve this in a chafing dish with cocktail picks, at cocktail parties.

This is the easiest way I know to prepare Elk or Deer; and it is by far the boys' favorite. Quite frankly, they prefer it to any Beef. Once when having company, I asked the boys if they would like "Teriyaki" Elk, as I had named it, and they quickly replied, "Yes", and turned to their friend and said, "Harry, you are going to LOVE it!". Now, that's the kind of praise I Love!

ELEGANT ELK RAGOUT

3 to 4 pounds boneless ELK Steak or Roast
3 tablespoons Oil
1/2 cup Onion, chopped fine
2 Garlic Cloves, chopped fine
1/4 cup Flour
4 Beef Bouillon Cubes
1 quart Water
1 Orange, sliced
1 Lemon, juiced

1 Bay Leaf
4 Cloves, whole
1/2 teaspoon Allspice
6 Peppercorns
3 tablespoons Fresh Parsley, minced
2 tablespoons Sherry Wine
1 tablespoon Orange Rind, grated
Salt and Pepper

Cut Elk meat into 1 inch cubes and saute in Oil, stirring frequently, until no longer pink in color.
Add Onion and Garlic and saute for additional 5 minutes.
Add Flour and blend well. Stir-in Bouillon Cubes and Water slowly to combine thoroughly.
Bring to a boil, then reduce temperature and continue simmering.
Add Orange Slices and Lemon Juice. In a cheesecloth bag, place Bay Leaf, Cloves, Allspice,
Peppercorns and Parsley; and lower tied bag into the stew pot.
Simmer until tender; about 1-1/2 to 2 hours.
Remove Orange Slices and Spice Bag. Add Sherry, Orange Rind and Salt and Pepper to taste.

ELEGANT ELK BIRDS

8 Elk or Deer Steaks
8 slices Boiled Ham, thin
8 slices Swiss Cheese, thin
2 tablespoons Oil
1 Garlic Clove, minced fine
1 Bay Leaf
12 small White Onions, peeled

1 cup White Chablis Wine
4 Fresh Tomatoes, peeled
1 tablespoon Flour
3 tablespoons Sherry Wine
Fresh Parsley
Salt and Pepper to taste

Individually, between sheets of waxed paper, pound steaks thin. Remove paper. Salt and Pepper Steaks.
Roll-up each Steak with slice of Ham and Cheese. Secure rolls with round toothpicks.
In large skillet, brown the 8 Elk Birds in Oil, and add crumbled Bay Leaf.
Remove Birds from Oil, add Onions and saute in skillet until soft; about 10 minutes.
Place Birds in a baking dish. Combine Wine and Garlic with Onions in skillet and pour over Birds.
Bake at 350 degrees for 35 to 40 minutes, with Whole Tomatoes surrounding Birds in baking dish.
Combine Sherry and Flour in pan juices, stir until blended. Pour over Birds, Onions and Tomatoes.
Garnish with Fresh Parsley for serving.
Serves 6 to 8.

DEER CANTONESE

1-1/2 pounds Deer Steak, sliced in thin strips
2 tablespoons Oil
2 cups diagonally sliced Celery
2 cups sliced Onion
1 package Fresh Spinach, Shredded
1 can mixed Chinese Vegetables

1 teaspoon Salt
1/8 teaspoon Pepper
1/4 cup Soy Sauce
1 twelve ounce can Beer
1 Garlic Clove, minced
Hot Cooked Rice

Brown Meat in Oil. Add Soy Sauce and Beer, Salt, Pepper, Garlic and Onions.
Simmer until tender; 1 to 2 hours.
Add Celery, Spinach and Chinese Vegetables during final 10 to 15 minutes. Do not overcook.
Allow added vegetables to remain crisp.
Serve over Hot Rice.
Serves 4 to 6.

DEER PICATTA

4 Deer Steaks, sliced very thin	2 tablespoons Butter
Flour	3 tablespoons Lemon Juice
Salt and Pepper	2 tablespoons Fresh Parsley, chopped
Oil	1 eight ounce package Spinach Noodles

Sprinkle Steaks with Flour, Salt and Pepper; then pound mixture into Steaks with edge of saucer.
Brown Steaks quickly in Hot Oil. Remove to warm platter and cover loosely. Reserve cooking mixture in skillet.
Prepare Noodles according to directions on package.
Add Lemon Juice and Parsley to skillet; add Butter. Heat and stir for sauce.
Arrange Meat slices on Noodles, topping with Butter Sauce. Garnish with fresh Lemon Slices and additional Parsley sprigs.

With a lovely tossed salad and White Wine, this is a romantic dinner for two!

ELK AND SAUSAGE PIE

1 pound Ground Elk	3 Sweet Italian Sausages
1/2 cup Bread Crumbs	2 Fresh Tomatoes
1 teaspoon Onion Powder	1 cup Grated Cheddar Cheese
1 nine inch unbaked Pie Shell	12 small Green Chile Peppers (canned)

Combine Ground Elk, Bread Crumbs and Onion Powder. Mix well, and press into Pie Shell.
Remove Sausages from casings, mash, and spread evenly over meat mixture, leaving 1/2 inch edge.
Bake at 350 degrees for 30 minutes. Remove from oven.
Peel and slice Tomatoes. Halve each slice and arrange around edge of pie. Sprinkle Tomatoes with
Grated Cheese. Arrange Chile Peppers spoke-fashion, inside circle of Tomatoes.
Return to oven at 350 degrees, for 10 minutes more.
Serve hot.

Different and Delicious!

ELK CHOUFLEUR

1 pound Elk or Deer Boneless Round,
                1/2 inch thick
1 small head Cauliflower
2 tablespoons Oil
1 Green Pepper, cut in strips
1/4 cup Soy Sauce

1 clove Garlic, minced
2 tablespoons Cornstarch
1/2 teaspoon Sugar
1-1/2 cup Beef Broth
1 cup Green Onions, sliced
Hot Cooked Rice

Cube Meat. Brown in Oil. Add Soy Sauce and cook until tender, adding water if necessary.
Separate Cauliflower into fleurettes.
Add Cauliflower, Green Pepper, Green Onion, Garlic and simmer until vegetables are tender;
about 10 minutes.
Blend Cornstarch, Sugar and Broth. Add to Meat mixture.
Cook, stirring constantly, to heat and thicken.
Serve over Hot Rice.
Serves 4 to 6.

ELK ORIENTAL

1 pound Elk Round Steak, 3/4 inch thick
1/4 cup Oil
1 cup Water
3 tablespoons Soy Sauce
1 Clove Garlic, minced
1 cup Carrots, diagonally sliced

1 cup Celery, diagonally sliced
2 cups Fresh Mushrooms, sliced
1/4 cup Cold Water
2 tablespoons Cornstarch
Hot Cooked Rice

Cut Meat into strips. Brown in Oil; drain.
Add Water, Soy Sauce and Garlic. Cover and simmer 45 to 55 minutes.
Add vegetables and cook an additional 15 to 20 minutes; allow vegetables to remain crisp.
Blend together Water and Cornstarch. Add mixture to Meat and Vegetables to thicken.
Serve over Hot Rice.
Serves 3 or 4.

ELK OR DEER WITH MUSHROOMS AND RED WINE

2 pounds Boneless Elk or Deer, cubed
3 Onions, sliced
2 tablespoons Oil
2 tablespoons Flour
Salt and Pepper

1 cup Red Wine
1/2 cup Beef Bouillon
1/2 cup Fresh Mushrooms, sliced
Hot Cooked Rice

Brown Meat in Oil.
Sprinkle with Flour and Seasonings. Stir-in half the Wine and the Beef Bouillon. Add Onions.
Simmer slowly for 2 to 3 hours, until tender; adding more Wine while cooking.
Add Mushrooms during final 30 minutes of cooking.
Serve over Hot Cooked Rice.
Serves 4 to 6.

ELK PASTITSIO GRECO

2 pounds Elk, ground
1 Onion, chopped
1 can (16 ounces) Tomatoes
1 can (6 ounces) Tomato Paste
1/4 teaspoon Thyme
2 cups Elbow Macaroni
4 Egg Whites, slightly beaten

1 cup Feta Cheese
1/2 cup Butter
1/2 cup Flour
1/4 teaspoon Cinnamon
4 cups Milk
4 Egg Yolks, slightly beaten

Brown Elk and Onion.
Add Tomatoes, Tomato Paste, Thyme and Salt. Simmer covered for 30 minutes, stirring often.
Cook Macaroni and drain. Add Egg Whites and Cheese to Macaroni, then stir-in Meat. Place in casserole.
In sauce pan, melt Butter; blend-in Flour, Cinnamon, 1 teaspoon Salt, and add Milk. Cook, stirring constantly until thick and bubbly.
Remove from heat and stir some of the hot sauce into the Egg Yolks. Blend well; then return the mixture to sauce, stirring rapidly.
Pour onto meat mixture in casserole and bake at 375 degrees for 35 to 40 minutes.
Let stand for 10 minutes before serving.
Serves 8 to 10.

ELK ROAST MILANO

3 pound Elk roast
1-1/2 teaspoons Salt
1/2 teaspoon Pepper
1 Garlic Clove, minced
3 tablespoons Oil
1 small can Tomato Paste

1 cup Chianti Wine
2 cups Water
1 Bouillon Cube
2 Onions, sliced
4 whole Cloves

Season Roast with Salt and Pepper. Brown in Oil in Dutch Oven.
Add Tomato Paste, Wine, Water, Bouillon Cube, Onions, Cloves and Garlic.
Cover and simmer until tender; about 1-1/2 to 2 hours.
Serve with a favorite Pasta (cooked).
Serves 6 to 8.

ELK SHISH KEBAB

3 to 4 pounds Elk Steak, cubed
1/2 bottle Beaujolais Wine
1/2 cup Oil
1 cup Vinegar
1/4 cup Worcestershire Sauce

2 tablespoons Onion Salt
1 tablespoon minced Garlic
3 tablespoons minced Parsley
1 Jalapeno Pepper
Fresh Tomatoes, Onions and Green Peppers

Cube Meat and marinate 5 to 6 hours, or overnight, in marinade made of combined seasonings listed above. Reserve Marinade.
Quarter tomatoes, Onions and slice Green Peppers. Thread on skewers, alternating meat and vegetables.
Grill over coals about an hour, or until cooked to taste; basting frequently with reserved marinade to which 12 ounces (1 can or bottle) of beer has been added. (May be broiled or cooked in oven)
Salt and Pepper to taste.
Serves 6 to 8.

ELK SUKIYAKI

2 pounds Elk Steak, cut into strips
Oil
Salt and Pepper
1 Garlic Clove, minced
1/4 cup Soy Sauce
2 tablespoons Oriental Brown Sauce
9 ounces (3/4 can) Beer
4 Green Onions, sliced

1 can Bean Sprouts - or 2 cups Fresh Bean Sprouts
1 Bell Pepper, sliced
1 cup Fresh Mushrooms, sliced
1 cup Celery, diagonally sliced
1 cup shredded Kohl-Rabi (or Cabbage)
2 cups shredded Fresh Spinach
Hot Cooked Rice

Brown Meat in Oil.
Add Salt, Pepper and Garlic, Soy Sauce, Brown Sauce and Beer.
Simmer 1-1/2 hours, until tender; adding more Beer if needed.
During the final 10 minutes, add vegetables. Avoid overcooking; allow vegetables to remain crisp.
Serve over Hot Rice.
Serves 4 to 6.

GREAT GROUSE

4 to 6 Grouse	Salt and Pepper
2 Onions, quartered	2 Garlic Cloves
4 Celery Ribs	Butter

Split Grouse through backs.
Place in large pot and add Water to cover the birds. Add Onions, Celery, Garlic and Salt and Pepper to taste. Cover and simmer for 30 minutes or until tender.
Remove birds from pot and place on broiler. Brush with Butter and baste frequently while cooking.
Broil for 15 minutes, turning once to brown evenly both sides.
Serves 4 to 6.

ROULADEN

3 pounds Elk or Deer Round Steak,
   sliced to 1/4 inch thickness
2 Onions, finely chopped
1 stick Butter or Margarine
1-1/2 pounds Fresh Mushrooms, chopped
3/4 pounds thinly sliced Cooked Ham

1 cup Dry Red Wine
1 cup Beef Bouillon
1 teaspoon Salt
Freshly Ground Black Pepper
2 tablespoons Cornstarch
2 tablespoons Cold Water
4 tablespoons Fresh Parsley, snipped

Remove all fat from Meat; pound Meat with wooden mallet, then cut into rectangles.
Saute Onions and half of Mushrooms in 4 tablespoons of Butter.
Place slice of Ham on each Meat slice, and fill with Onion and Mushroom stuffing. Roll up, jelly-roll fashion, and secure with round toothpicks.
Melt Butter and brown the Meat-rolls in heavy skillet. Pour in Wine, Bouillon, and season with Salt and Pepper. Cover and simmer about 15 minutes; then place Meat-rolls into a casserole.
Bring juices to a boil, then add Cornstarch and Water until thickened. Add balance of Mushrooms.
Pour this sauce over Meat-rolls and bake at 375 degrees for 40 minutes or until tender.
Sprinkle with Fresh Parsley Snips.

Serve with Red Cabbage and Dumplings or Boiled Potatoes.
Accompany with a dry Rhine Wine.

GOURMET STEAK

Deer or Elk Steaks
    or Ground Meat Patties
2/3 cup Soy Sauce
2 tablespoons Water

2/3 cup Sugar
1 teaspoon Sherry
1 Garlic Clove
Dash ground Ginger

Combine sauce ingredients and bring to a boil. Lower heat and simmer for 5 minutes. Use as a basting sauce to grill Steaks or Ground Meat Patties.

This is a very simple sauce to make, but one which adds excitement to broiled Meat.

MOUSSAKA

2 medium Eggplants, peeled and sliced
   to 1-1/2 inch thickness
1 pound Elk or Deer, ground
1 Onion, chopped
1/4 cup Burgundy Wine
3 tablespoons Fresh Parsley, snipped
1 tablespoon Tomato Paste
2/3 cup soft Breadcrumbs

3 Eggs, beaten
1 cup Cheddar Cheese, grated
Dash ground Cinnamon
3 tablespoons Butter
3 tablespoons Flour
1-1/2 cups Milk
Dash ground Nutmeg
Oil

Salt Eggplant slices on both sides, then press between paper towels under weight, for 30 minutes.
Brown Meat and Onions in 2 tablespoons Oil. Add Burgundy, Parsley, Tomato Paste, 1/4 cup of
Water, 1 teaspoon Salt and dash of Black Pepper. Simmer until liquid is nearly absorbed. Cool.
Stir-in half the Breadcrumbs, 2 beaten Eggs, 1/2 cup grated Cheese and Cinnamon.
Melt Butter in sauce pan. Add Flour and Milk, stirring constantly until thick and bubbly.
Add Nutmeg, 1/2 teaspoon Salt and dash of Pepper. Add small amount of sauce to one beaten
Egg, mix and return to hot mixture. Continue cooking, and stir over low heat for 2 minutes.
Brown Eggplant slices on both sides in a small amount of Oil.
Sprinkle bottom of 2 quart casserole with remaining Breadcrumbs. Cover with half of Eggplant,
and spoon-on Meat mixture. Arrange remainder of Eggplant on top and pour prepared sauce over it.
Top with remaining Cheese and bake at 350 degrees for 45 minutes.
Serves 6 to 8.

HAWAIIAN JERKY

3 pounds Elk or Deer Steak   1/2 teaspoon Salt
1/2 cup Soy Sauce   1/4 teaspoon Garlic Powder

Trim fat from Meat and cut into long, very thin strips about 2 inches wide.
Place in a shallow, long dish.
Combine remaining ingredients and pour over Meat. Marinate 4 hours.
Preheat oven to 275 degrees. Place Meat strips on cooling racks set on baking sheets.
Bake for 3 hours, or until adequately dried.

Great trail food! Or for snacks.

HEARTY HUNGARIAN SOUP

3 pounds Elk or Deer, cubed
2 tablespoons Oil
2 tablespoons Butter
2 large Onions, chopped
1 Garlic Clove, minced
1 tablespoon Paprika
1 teaspoon Caraway Seeds
5 cups Water

1 Bell Pepper, seeded and
  cut into strips
2 teaspoons Salt
1/8 teaspoon Pepper
2 Tomatoes, peeled, seeded
  and coarsely chopped
1 small Dried Chile, crushed
2 Potatoes, cut into eighths

Brown Meat in Oil in a large skillet.
Melt Butter in soup kettle and saute Onions and Garlic. Then add Paprika and Caraway Seeds.
Add browned Meat, Water, Bell Pepper, Tomatoes and red hot Chile.
Bring to a boil, reduce heat, cover and simmer for 2 hours or until Meat is tender.
Cool soup slightly and add Potatoes. Cover and cook 20 to 30 minutes longer until Potatoes are done.
Serve piping hot on a cold Winter day.
Serves 6.

HUNTER'S STEW

2 to 3 pounds Deer or Elk, cubed
1 Onion, chopped
2 stalks Celery, chopped
2 Chile Peppers
3 tablespoons Fresh Parsley, minced
1 teaspoon Oregano

1/2 cup Vinegar
3 Fresh Tomatoes
4 or 5 Potatoes, quartered
4 or 5 Carrots, sliced lengthwise
     into strips
4 ounces Sherry

Dredge Meat in Flour and brown in a small amount of Oil.
Add Onions, Celery, Chile Peppers, Seasonings and braise.
Add Vinegar, Vegetables and Sherry.
Cook 1 to 2 hours over low heat until tender. Add water if necessary.
Serves 6.

INDIA SHISH-KEBABS

2 pounds Elk or Deer, cubed to 1-1/2 inches
2/3 cup Dry Red Wine
1/4 cup Oil
1/4 cup Fresh Parsley, minced
1/2 cup Onion, grated
2 Garlic cloves

1 teaspoon Salt
1 Bay Leaf
1/8 teaspoon Black Pepper
2 Green Bell Peppers
3 Fresh Tomatoes
2 Onions

Mix Wine, Oil, Parsley, one Onion, sliced, seasonings and Garlic cloves.
Add Meat to marinade. Marinate overnight in refrigerator, turning to coat all Meat.
Drain Meat and reserve marinade.
Clean and quarter Bell Peppers, Tomatoes and Onion. Place on skewers, alternating Meat cubes and vegetables.
Cook over open grill or Broil in oven, basting with marinade until done.
Serve over Rice Pilaf.

This is a festive dish when served with a fresh fruit cup salad and Lime Sherbet for dessert.
Add a crisp, dry Red Wine and you have an elegant meal.

ITALIAN SPAGHETTI

1-1/2 pounds Elk or Deer, ground
1 teaspoon Worcestershire Sauce
2 teaspoons Red Wine Vinegar Salad Dressing
1 Garlic Clove, minced
1/3 teaspoon Salt
1/4 teaspoon Pepper
1 large Onion, chopped
1 Green Bell Pepper, chopped
1 number 2 can Tomatoes

1 can Tomatoes with Green Chiles
1 can Tomato Paste
1 teaspoon Oregano
2 cans Whole Mushrooms
1 small can Ripe Olives, sliced
1/2 bottle Catsup, regular size
3/4 cup Sharp Cheese, grated
1 teaspoon Baking Soda
Spaghetti

Mix together Meat, Worcestershire Sauce, Red Wine Vinegar Salad Dressing, Garlic Cloves, Salt and Pepper. Allow the mixture to stand for 1 to 2 hours.
Saute Onion and Bell Bepper in Oil. Add Tomatoes, Tomato Paste and Oregano. Simmer 2 hours.
Brown Meat mixture in Oil, add to sauce and cook an additional 30 minutes.
Add Mushrooms, Olives, Cheese, Catsup and Salt and Pepper to taste. Add Baking Soda and continue cooking until Soda stops "fizzing".
Cook Spaghetti according to directions on package.
Serve with Meat mixture; topping it with grated Parmesan Cheese.
Serves 4 to 6.

JUDY'S FAMOUS SWISS STEAK

2 to 3 pounds Deer or Elk Steak
1/2 cup Flour
1 teaspoon Salt
1/2 teaspoon Pepper
1/3 cup Oil

2 cups sliced Onions
1 #2 can Tomatoes
1 Bell Pepper, seeded and sliced
1/2 teaspoon Thyme
1 Bay Leaf

Mix Flour, Salt and Pepper. Flour both sides of Steak and pound with wooden mallet.
Brown Steak in hot Oil about 20 minutes, adding Onion during last 5 minutes.
Add Tomatoes, 1/2 cup Water, Peppers, Thyme and Bay Leaf.
Bring to a boil. Reduce heat and simmer covered for 1 Hour.
Turn steak and simmer 1 hour longer or until tender.
Serves 4 to 6.

JACKSON LAKE MACKINAW OR CUT-THROAT TROUT

4 to 6 freshly caught Mackinaw   2 or 3 Lemons
Oil   1 cup Shallots, chopped
Salt and Pepper   Teriyaki Sauce
Paprika

Place Fish on large piece of heavy-duty foil.
Coat Fish with Oil and season to taste with Salt, Pepper, Paprika, Lemon Juice, Shallots and
Teriyaki Sauce.
Place on grill over hot coals and cover loosely with separate piece of foil. Cook about 15 minutes.
Uncover, turn, and season. Cover again and cook an additional 15 minutes.
Serve immediately.
Serves 4 to 6.

Always remember; do not overcook Fish.

MACKINAW OR CUT-THROAT TROUT PROVENCALE

4 to 6 whole, small Trout
1/3 cup Olive Oil
1/4 cup Shallots, chopped
1/2 cup Bell Pepper, chopped
1/4 cup Fresh Lemon Juice

3 tablespoons Fresh Parsley, minced
4 Fresh Tomatoes, peeled and chopped
4 ounces Tomato Sauce
1/4 cup Stuffed Olives, sliced
Lemon Slices

Brown Shallots and Bell Peppers lightly in Olive Oil. Remove from pan.
Brown Fish on both sides in Oil.
Place Fish in large casserole dish.
Remove excess Oil from skillet and add Shallots, Bell Peppers, Salt, Pepper, Lemon Juice and Parsley; then add Fresh Tomatoes and Tomato Sauce. Simmer a few minutes to blend.
Pour over Fish in casserole and bake at 350 degrees about 15 minutes, until Fish flakes easily.
Do not overcook.
Garnish with Stuffed Olive and Lemon slices.
Serves 4.

MARVELOUS MANICOTTI

1 pound Deer or Elk, ground
1/4 cup Bell Pepper, chopped
2 cans Tomatoes
2 cans Tomato Sauce
2 tablespoons Butter

1/2 teaspoon Garlic Salt
1 Onion, finely chopped
8 Manicotti Shells
1/2 pound Mozzarella cheese, grated
Parmesan Cheese, grated

Mix together Tomatoes, Tomato Sauce, Butter and Garlic Salt. Cover and simmer 25 minutes.
Cook Manicotti Shells in boiling water about 7 minutes. Drain.
Brown Meat and Bell Peppers; remove from heat and stir-in Mozzarells Cheese.
Stuff Meat mixture into Manicotti Shells.
Pour half the sauce into baking dish. Place stuffed Manicotti on top, and cover with remaining sauce.
Sprinkle with grated Parmesan Cheese and bake at 375 degrees for 30 minutes.
Serves 4.

DEER SAUSAGE QUICHE

1 ten inch Pie Shell
1 can (7 ounce size) Green Chiles
1 pound Deer Sausage
4 Eggs, slightly beaten

2 cups Light Cream
1/2 cup Parmesan Cheese, grated
3/4 cup Swiss Cheese, grated
Salt and Pepper to taste

Line uncooked Pie Shell with split and seeded whole Green Chiles.
Cook Deer Sausage, pour off grease, cool and crumble; then sprinkle over Chiles in Pie Shell.
Combine Eggs, Cream, Cheeses, Salt and Pepper uniformly, and pour mixture into Pie Shell.
Bake at 350 degrees for 30 to 40 minutes, until golden brown and set.
Remove from oven and allow to sit for 5 minutes before serving.
Serves 6 to 8.

MEXICALI BAKE

1-1/2 pounds Deer or Elk, ground
2 tablespoons Oil
1 Onion, chopped
1 tablespoon Flour
1 can Tomato Paste
1 teaspoon Salt

1 teaspoon Chili Powder
1/4 teaspoon Black Pepper
1 cup Cheddar Cheese, grated
1/2 cup Ripe Olives, sliced
1 package (18 ounces) Corn Muffin Mix

Brown Meat in Oil, adding Onion. Stir-in Flour, add Tomato Paste, Salt, Chili Powder and Pepper.
Remove from heat. Add Cheese and Olives.
Spread evenly over bottom of 9 by 9 by 2 inch square baking pan.
Prepare Muffin Mix according to package directions and spread over Meat mixture in pan.
Bake in preheated oven at 400 degrees for 30 to 40 minutes.
Let set for 5 minutes, then loosen edges and invert on serving platter.
Serves 8.

A quick one the kids like.

MOCK FILET MIGNON

Elk or Deer, ground
Bacon slices
Salt and Pepper

Garlic Powder
Worcestershire Sauce

Shape meat thickly into desired number of patties. Wrap slice or two of Bacon around patties and secure with round toothpicks.
Broil on charcoal grill or in over broiler.
During cooking, sprinkle with Worcestershire Sauce and season to taste with Garlic Powder, Salt and Pepper.

Simple! And serves any number deliciously!

MOUNTAIN MEAT-PIE

1 pound Deer or Elk, ground
4 ounces Tomato Sauce
1/2 cup Bread Crumbs
1/4 cup Onion, chopped
1/4 cup Bell Pepper, chopped
1 teaspoon Salt

1/4 teaspoon Black Pepper
1 Garlic Clove, minced
1 teaspoon Worcestershire Sauce
1 cup Rice
2-1/2 cans (8 ounce size) Tomato Sauce
1 cup Cheddar Cheese, grated

Combine Meat, Tomato Sauce, Bread Crumbs, Onion, Bell Pepper, Salt, Pepper, Garlic and Worcestershire Sauce.
Pat this mixture into the bottom and sides of a greased 9 inch pie pan.
Boil Rice in 2 cups Water until half-cooked; about 10 minutes.
Combine Rice, Cooking Water, Tomato Sauce (1 can), and 1/4 cup grated Cheese. Place in Meat shell.
Cover with foil and bake at 350 degrees for 25 minutes.
Pour-off excess juices. Sprinkle with remaining Cheese that has been combined with 1/2 can Tomato Sauce; and bake uncovered for 15 minutes longer.
Cut into pie-shaped wedges to serve.
Serves 4 to 6.

The children love it!

POLISH STUFFED CABBAGE LEAVES

1 pound Elk or Deer, ground
1/3 cup Rice
1 head Cabbage
1 Egg
1/2 Onion, finely chopped

1/2 teaspoon Salt
dash Pepper
1 #2 can Tomatoes
2 eight ounce cans Tomato Sauce
1 Bay Leaf

Cook Rice according to package directions.
Remove 8 outer leaves from head of Cabbage.
Shred 4 cups of Cabbage and place in bottom of large baking dish. Salt.
Dip the reserved 8 Cabbage leaves in boiling Water to make them limp.
Combine cooked Rice, slightly beaten Egg, ground Deer or Elk, chopped Onion, Salt and Pepper
and mix well. Then add one can of Tomato Sauce.
Divide mixture evenly and fill Cabbage Leaves. Fold over and make roll, seam side down. Secure
with round toothpicks as necessary. Place in baking dish atop the shredded Cabbage.
Mix canned Tomatoes, other can of Tomato Sauce and Bay leaf in sauce pan.
Simmer 5 minutes and pour over Cabbage rolls.
Cover and bake 1 to 1-1/2 hours at 325 degrees.
Serves 4.

PEACH BLOSSOM GROUSE OR QUAIL

4 Grouse or 12 Quail
Salt and Pepper
3 cups Barbecue Sauce
2 Onions, chopped
1 ten ounce jar Peach Preserves

2 tablespoons Soy Sauce
1 six ounce can Water Chestnuts
2 Green Bell Peppers
Hot Fluffy Rice

Place halved Grouse or split Quail skin side up in a large, shallow baking pan.
Salt and Pepper Birds to taste. Add a small amount of Water to bottom of pan to prevent sticking.
Combine Barbecue Sauce, Onion, Preserves and Soy Sauce. Spoon over Birds.
Cover and bake at 350 degrees for 30 minutes.
Turn Birds and spoon-on additional Sauce. Cover and bake another 30 minutes.
Turn again, skin side up, and coat with remaining Sauce. Bake uncovered another 30 minutes.
Add drained, sliced Water Chestnuts and sliced Bell Peppers. Cook for final 10 minutes.
The Birds should be tender and nicely browned.
Serves 6.

QUAIL EN BROCHETTE WITH EGGPLANT

8 to 10 Quail Breasts, boned
1 cup Eggplant, peeled and cut to 1" cubes
1/2 cup Oil
1 teaspoon Beef Bouillon

1/4 cup Sherry Wine
1 teaspoon Catsup
1 teaspoon Garlic Salt
1/2 teaspoon Black Pepper

For marinade, combine Oil, Bouillon, Sherry, Catsup, Garlic Salt and Pepper.
Marinate Quail Breasts 8 hours, turning occasionally.
Place Quail and Eggplant cubes alternately on skewers.
Broil on charcoal grill until nicely browned, about 25 minutes.
Baste frequently and turn, while cooking.
Serves 4.

PHEASANT OR GROUSE WHIZ

2 cups cooked Pheasant or Grouse, cubed
1/2 Onion, chopped
1/4 cup Butter or Oil
1 ten ounce box frozen, chopped Broccoli
   or 1 cup Fresh Broccoli, chopped
1/2 can Mushroom Soup, undiluted

1 eight ounce jar Cheez-Whiz
1 two ounce jar Pimiento, chopped
Salt and Pepper to taste
Paprika
3 teaspoons slivered Almonds

Cook frozen Broccoli according to package directions, or cook fresh Broccoli until tender, yet crisp.
Drain and arrange Broccoli in bottom of shallow 9 by 9 inch casserole.
Layer Pheasant or Grouse over Broccoli, and Salt and Pepper to taste.
Saute Onion in Butter or Oil, add Mushroom Soup, Cheez-Whiz, Pimientos and mix thoroughly.
Pour over Broccoli-Meat mixture.
Sprinkle with Paprika and Almonds and bake at 350 degrees for 20 to 25 minutes.
Serves 4.

This is an excellent way to serve leftover Fried Birds.

PARTY STROGANOFF MEATBALLS

1 pound Elk or Deer, ground
2 tablespoons Oil
1 cup Beef Bouillon
1 cup Sour Cream
1/4 cup Sherry
1 teaspoon Marjoram

1/4 cup dry Bread Crumbs
1 Egg, beaten
1 teaspoon Salt
1/4 teaspoon Black Pepper
1 Garlic Clove, minced

Combine, Meat, Bread Crumbs, Egg, Salt, Pepper and Garlic. Shape into balls.
Brown in Oil.
Add Bouillon and simmer to absorb liquid, turning frequently.
Add Sour Cream, Sherry and Marjoram.

Adjust quantities to serve a crowd.

ROAST PHEASANT

4 Pheasants
Salt and Pepper
2 Onions, chopped

4 Garlic Cloves
1 Lemon
Dry White Wine
8 Bacon slices

Salt and Pepper each Bird.
Inside cavity of each, place 2 teaspoons chopped Onion, Garlic Clove and 1 Lemon slice.
Secure legs and place in pan, breast-side up. Place 2 strips of Bacon over each Bird.
Add 1/2 bottle Dry White Wine.
Roast at 325 degrees for 1-1/2 hours or until tender, adding more Wine if necessary.
Baste often during roasting.
Serves 4.

ROAST WILD DUCK

2 Ducks, 2 to 3 pounds each   Salt and Pepper
1 Onion, quartered   Dry White Wine
2 Apples, quartered   Bacon slices

Stuff cavity of Ducks with Onions and Apples. Salt and Pepper to taste.
Add 1/2 bottle of Dry White Wine.
Place 2 Bacon strips criss-crossed over breast of each Duck.
Bake uncovered at 400 degrees for 4 to 5 hours, until tender.
Baste often; adding more Wine if necessary.

ROCKY MOUNTAIN BURGUNDY RAGOUT

2 pounds Elk or Deer Steak
2 tablespoons Oil
1 teaspoon Thyme
1 Bay Leaf
1 Garlic Clove, minced

1 can Tomato Sauce
1 package Fresh Mushrooms, sliced
1 cup Burgundy Wine
1 cup Carrots, sliced
Salt and Pepper

Cube Meat and brown in Oil in heavy skillet.
Add Thyme, Bay Leaf and Garlic. Then add Tomato Sauce and Burgundy.
Cover and simmer 2-1/2 hours.
Add Mushrooms and Carrots and simmer until tender; about 1/2 hour.
Salt and Pepper to taste.
Serves 6.

RUSSIAN STROGANOFF

1 pound Elk or Deer Steak,
  cut into thin strips
1 tablespoon Flour
1/2 teaspoon Salt
4 tablespoons Butter
1/2 pound Fresh Mushrooms
1/2 cup Onion, chopped
1 Garlic Clove, minced

2 tablespoons Butter
3 tablespoons Flour
1 tablespoon Tomato Paste
1 can (10-1/2 ounce) Beef Broth or
  1 Bouillon Cube in Hot Water
1 cup Sour Cream
1/4 cup Dry White Wine
Hot Buttered Noodles

Coat Meat with 1 tablespoon Flour and half-teaspoon Salt.
Brown Meat quickly in 2 tablespoons Butter.
Add Mushrooms, Onion and Garlic. Cook until tender, 3 to 4 minutes. Remove Meat and Mushrooms.
Add 2 tablespoons Butter to pan drippings and blend in 3 tablespoons Flour. Add Tomato Paste and stir-in Beef Broth.
Cook over medium heat, stirring until sauce is thick and bubbly.
Return Meat and Mushrooms to skillet, then stir-in Sour Cream and Wine.
Cook slowly. Do not boil.
Serve over Hot Buttered Noodles.
Serves 4.

SAUSAGE PATTIES

Elk or Deer Sausage, ground   Oil

Shape Meat into patties. Cook in skillet in small amount of Oil
Salt and Pepper to taste. Serve with Eggs of your choice.

SAUSAGE PINWHEELS

Elk or Deer Bulk Sausage   Biscuit Mix

Make 3 batches of biscuits according to directions. Roll each separately as in making pie crust.
Spread each with 1/3 pound of Sausage Meat. Roll up jelly-roll style. Slice into "cookies".
Place pinwheels on greased baking sheet.
Bake at 375 degrees for 10 minutes or until lightly browned.

Great for brunch or with cocktails!

SICILIAN MEAT LOAF

1 pound Elk or Deer, ground
1 Garlic Clove, minced
1/2 cup Onion, chopped
1/2 cup Tomato Sauce
1/4 cup Dry Bread Crumbs
1 teaspoon Salt

1/4 teaspoon Black Pepper
1 Egg, beaten
4 slices Cheddar Cheese, cut into strips
1/4 cup Stuffed Green Olives, sliced
1/4 cup Ripe Olives, sliced

Mix Meat, Garlic, Onion, Tomato Sauce, Bread Crumbs, Salt, Pepper and Egg.
Shape into a round patty on baking sheet.
Bake at 350 degrees for 45 minutes to 1 hour, pouring-off any excess fat.
Arrange Cheese and Olive slices on top. Return to oven and bake 5 minutes more.
Serves 4.

SKIERS' SPECIAL STEW

3 to 4 pounds Deer or Elk, cubed
Flour
Oil
1-1/2 cup Water
1-1/4 cup Burgundy Wine
4 or 5 Potatoes, quartered

1/2 teaspoon each Thyme, Marjoram, Parsley Flakes
1 teaspoon Salt
1/2 teaspoon Black Pepper
1 Onion
2 large Carrots

Flour Meat, brown in Oil in pressure cooker.
Add Water, Wine, Herbs, Vegetables and Seasonings.
Place cover and regulator on cooker and cook 25 minutes with regulator rocking.
(Preheat pressure cooker to prevent sticking).
Serves 4.

This is quick and easy to prepare after a day on the slopes!

SUPER SHISH KEBAB

3 to 4 pounds Deer or Elk Steak, cubed
1/2 bottle Burgundy or Beaujolais Wine
1/2 cup Oil
1 cup Vinegar
1/4 cup Worcestershire Sauce
2 tablespoons Onion Salt
1 tablespoon Garlic, minced

3 tablespoons Fresh Parsley, minced
1 Jalapeno Pepper, canned
3 Fresh Tomatoes
2 Onions
2 Bell Peppers
1 can (12 ounces) Beer

Mix Wine, Oil, Vinegar, Worcestershire Sauce, Onion Salt, Garlic, Parsley and Jalapeno Pepper to make marinade.
Marinate cubed Meat at least 5 hours or preferably, overnight, turning occasionally.
Reserve marinade.
Quarter Tomatoes, Onions and seeded Bell Peppers and thread alternately with Meat on skewers.
Grill over coals for 1 hour, basting frequently with reserved marinade to which 1 can of Beer has been added. Season with Black Pepper and Garlic Salt to taste.
Serve over Hot, Fluffy Rice.

Serves 6 to 8.

SWEET AND PUNGENT MEATBALLS

1 pound Elk or Deer, ground
2 tablespoons Onion, minced
1 Egg
1/4 cup dry Bread Crumbs
1/2 teaspoon Salt
1/8 teaspoon Black Pepper

1 cup Beef Bouillon
3 tablespoons Brown Sugar
3 tablespoons Soy Sauce
1/4 cup Vinegar
1/2 cup Catsup

Mix ground Elk or Deer with Minced Onion, slightly beaten Egg, Bread Crumbs, Salt and Pepper.
Blend ingredients well and shape into 1 inch diameter Meat Balls.
Heat Bouillon until boiling, add Meat Balls and simmer covered, about 30 minutes.
Combine Brown Sugar, Soy Sauce, Vinegar and Catsup.
Add to Meat Balls and simmer about 15 minutes more.
Serves 4 to 6.

SWEET AND SOUR DEER STEAK

2 pounds Deer Steak
1 teaspoon Salt
1/4 teaspoon Black Pepper
1/4 cup Flour

2 tablespoons Oil
1 cup Sugar
3/4 cup Vinegar
1/4 cup Soy Sauce

Preheat oven to 350 degrees.
Score and pound Steak. Sprinkle with Salt and Pepper; then coat with Flour.
Heat Oil and brown Meat.
Place in baking pan.
Combine Sugar, Vinegar and Soy Sauce in small saucepan, and bring to a boil.
Pour sauce over Meat and bake uncovered for 1 hour.
Serves 4.

SWEET AND SOUR RIBS

3 to 4 pounds Deer Ribs
1 medium size bottle Catsup
2 tablespoons Worcestershire Sauce
Dash Tabasco
Dash Black Pepper

Juice of one Lemon
Dash Garlic Powder
1/2 cup Red Wine Vinegar
1/3 cup White Karo Syrup

Combine sauce ingredients and stir thoroughly; then coat Ribs generously.
Cook in covered pan at 350 degrees until tender; then uncover and brown for an additional 30 minutes cooking time.
These may also be cooked on the grill, basting often with sauce.
Serves 4 to 6.

TERIYAKI ELK

2 pounds boneless Elk,
  cut into strips
1/2 cup Onion, finely chopped
2 tablespoons Sugar
1/2 teaspoon Ginger, ground

1 Garlic Clove, minced
2 tablespoons Peanut Oil
1/2 cup Soy Sauce
1/4 cup Sherry Wine

Combine Onion, Sugar, Ginger, Garlic, Oil, Soy Sauce and Sherry; stirring well.
Mix in Meat strips, coating all thoroughly. Cover, and refrigerate several hours or overnight.
Thread strips of Elk on metal skewers and broil 3 inches from heat; 2 to 3 minutes each side.
Serves 4.

TERIYAKI MEATBALLS

1 pound Elk or Deer, ground
1/4 cup Onion, chopped
1/4 cup Flour
1 Egg
1 teaspoon Salt
1/4 teaspoon Black Pepper
1/4 cup Soy Sauce

1 tablespoon Oil
3 teaspoons Sherry Wine
1/2 cup Water
2 tablespoons Brown Sugar
1/8 teaspoon Ginger, ground
1 teaspoon Garlic Salt
2 teaspoons Cornstarch

Combine Meat, Onion, Flour, Egg, Salt, Pepper and 1 tablespoon Soy Sauce. Shape mixture into Meatballs.
Heat Oil and fry Meatballs until lightly browned.
Combine Soy Sauce, Sherry, Water, Brown Sugar, Ginger, Garlic Salt and Cornstarch.
Add Meatballs and cook on low heat until sauce thickens.
Yield, 4 dozen.

VENISON SAUSAGE AND LENTIL CASSEROLE

2 pounds Venison Sausage
1 cup Lentils, dried
2 tablespoons Oil
2 cups Onion, chopped
2 Garlic Cloves, minced
1 Fresh Carrot, grated

2 or 3 Fresh Tomatoes, chopped
1 teaspoon Sugar
1/2 teaspoon Black Pepper
1/2 teaspoon Salt
1 Bay Leaf

Cook Lentils in a saucepan; bringing to a boil, then reducing heat. Simmer 20 minutes. Drain, reserving liquid.
Saute Onions and Garlic in Oil. Then add Carrots and Tomatoes.
Slice Sausage about 1/8 inch thick and brown slices in Oil.
Place all ingredients in casserole, adding Sugar, Pepper, Salt and Bay Leaf. Stir.
Bake at 350 degrees for 30 minutes. Add more Lentil liquid if too dry.
Serves 4.

ROSS' VENISON ROAST

4 to 5 pound Deer Roast
Salt
Black Pepper

Garlic Cloves
Celery Salt
1 medium Onion , quartered

Meat may be soaked an hour or so in Salt or Soda Water to mellow the wild taste, if desired.
Preheat oven to 375 degrees.
Brown Roast very lightly in a small amount of Bacon Grease or Oil.
Add seasonings, spiking Meat with slivers of Garlic.
Place in roaster pan and add 3 to 4 cups Water. Place Onion pieces on top and around Roast.
Cook 3 to 4 hours, to desired taste.
(The Deer Roast is not as tasty rare as it is more well-done.)

For a really great Venison Roast, I asked Maxine Ross to share her recipe with you. Her husband
is quite a hunter and she can really cook the game to perfection.

VENISON ENCHILADAS

1 pound Ground Venison
1 dozen Tortillas
1 large Onion, chopped finely
1 tablespoon Chili Powder

Salt and Pepper
1 can (eight ounces) Tomato Sauce
1 can (ten ounces) Chili, without beans
1 pound Cheddar Cheese, grated

Brown Meat in 2 tablespoons Oil.
Add 1/4 cup Onion, Chili Powder and Salt and Pepper to taste. Then add Tomato Sauce, 2 cups Water and Chili. Simmer for 20 minutes.
Dip Tortillas in Hot Oil and fill each Tortilla with 1 teaspoon Onion, 2 tablespoons Grated Cheese and 1 tablespoon Chili mixture.
Roll up and place seam-side down in casserole. Top with additional Onion, Chili mixture and Grated Cheese.
Bake at 350 degrees for 15 minutes.
Serves 4 to 6.

WILD DUCKS BURGUNDY

2 Ducks, quartered
2 tablespoons Oil
2 tablespoons Flour
1 cup Beef Bouillon
1 cup Fresh Mushrooms, sliced
1/2 cup Burgundy Wine

2 tablespoons Shallots
1/2 teaspoon Salt
1/4 teaspoon Black Pepper
1 Garlic Clove
1/4 cup Fresh Parsley, minced
Paprika

Simmer Ducks in a large saucepan in small amount of Salted Water for 30 minutes. Drain.
In a large skillet, brown Ducks in Oil.
Remove Ducks and place in a suitable baking dish.
Blend Flour into skillet juices, add Bouillon, Mushrooms, Burgundy, Shallots, Salt, Pepper and Garlic.
Cook, stirring frequently, until thick and bubbly.
Pour sauce over Ducks in baking dish, cover and bake until tender; about 1-1/2 hours.
Place Ducks on platter, skim off fat, and pour sauce over Ducks.
Sprinkle with Parsley and Paprika.
Serves 3 or 4.

WYOMING WAPITI*

1 to 2 pounds Elk Round Steak,
    thinly sliced
1/4 cup Flour
Salt and Pepper
3 tablespoons Oil

1 cup Green Onions, chopped
1/2 to 1 cup Burgundy Wine
2 Beef Bouillon Cubes
1 cup Fresh Mushrooms, sliced
3 cups Hot Cooked Rice

Cut Meat into 1 inch strips. Coat with Flour and add Salt and Pepper to taste.
Brown in Oil. Add Onions and cook 2 to 3 minutes longer.
Stir-in Wine, Bouillon Cubes and Mushrooms; and bring to a boil.
Cover, reduce heat, and simmer 2 hours or until tender; adding more Wine if necessary.
Serve over Hot Cooked Rice.
Garnish serving platter with Fresh Tomato Wedges and Fresh Parsley sprigs.
Serves 4.

    * Wapiti is the Shawnee Indian name for Elk!

WOK MELANGE

2 to 3 pounds Deer or Elk Steak, slivered
3 tablespoons Oil
1 teaspoon Worcestershire Sauce
3 tablespoons Soy Sauce
2 teaspoons Sherry Wine
2 Garlic Cloves, minced
Salt and Pepper
1/2 cup Shallots, chopped

1 cup Celery, sliced diagonally
1 cup Fresh Mushrooms, sliced
1 Bell Pepper, seeded and sliced into strips
1 cup Fresh Broccoli, separated
   into fleurettes
1 cup Cabbage, shredded
2 teaspoons Cornstarch
Hot Cooked Rice

Place 2 tablespoons Oil, Worcestershire Sauce, 2 tablespoons Soy Sauce and Garlic into Chinese Wok on high heat.
Add Meat, stirring and cooking until all liquid is absorbed and Meat is thoroughly browned. Add Sherry.
Transfer Meat from wok to platter.
Pour the remaining Oil and Soy Sauce into wok on high heat. Add Vegetables and cook 7 minutes.
Stir constantly to prevent sticking. Then, add Cornstarch to mixture in wok.
Return Meat to wok and blend with Vegetables. Salt and Pepper to taste.
Serve over Hot Cooked Rice.
Serves 5 or 6.

ZUCCHINI-ELK SPAGHETTI

1 pound Elk or Deer, ground
2 tablespoons Oil
1 Garlic Clove, Minced
1 pound small Fresh Zucchini, sliced
1 cup Green Bell Pepper, sliced

2 Fresh Tomatoes, peeled and quartered
1 teaspoon Salt
1/4 teaspoon Black Pepper
8 ounces Spaghetti, cooked and drained

Heat Oil. Add Meat and Garlic and cook until browned.
Add Zucchini, Green Peppers, Tomatoes, Salt and Pepper.
Cook over low heat about 30 minutes.
Serve Meat and Vegetable Sauce over Hot Spaghetti.
Serves 4.

UNUSUAL ACCOMPANIMENTS TO WILD GAME

"May I offer you some adventuresome recipes for perfect accompaniments to your special entrees? You will find some really good ideas to serve with your wild game."

APRICOT-NUT RICE

1/2 cup boiling Chicken Broth or
    Chicken Bouillon (1 cube)
1 cup Dried Apricots, chopped
1 cup Shallots, chopped
2 cups Celery, sliced diagonally

3 tablespoons Butter
3 cups Cooked Rice
1/2 cup Pecans, chopped
3/4 cup Poultry Seasoning (optional)
Salt and Pepper to taste

Add chopped Dried Apricots to boiling Chicken Broth.
Saute Shallots and Celery in Butter, and add to Apricot mixture.
Then, stir-in Cooked Rice, Pecans, Poultry Seasoning, Salt and Pepper.
Place in casserole dish and bake at 350 degrees for 20 minutes.
Yield: 20 cups.

ARTICHOKE HEART CURRY SALAD

1 package Long Grain and Wild Rice mix
1 teaspoon Chicken Bouillon powder
2 jars (6 ounce size) Artichoke Hearts
5 Green Shallots, chopped

1/2 cup Bell Pepper, chopped
1/3 cup Stuffed Olives, chopped
3/4 teaspoon Curry Powder
1/3 cup Mayonnaise

Cook Rice according to package directions, including Bouillon in cooking Water. Cool.
Drain and chop Artichoke Hearts, and reserve liquid.
Combine liquid, Curry Powder and Mayonnaise, and set aside.
To Rice, add Shallots, Bell Pepper and Oilves. Mix well.
Add and stir-in Mayonnaise mixture to distribute evenly. Chill to serve.
For superior flavor, make 24 hours ahead of serving.

STUFFED ARTICHOKES

4 Fresh Artichokes
1 stick Butter
2 cups Bread Crumbs

3/4 cup Green Onions, chopped
Salt and Pepper to taste
1 cup Parmesan Cheese, grated

Clip sharp tips from Artichoke Leaves with kitchen shears, and trim stems so Artichoke will sit level.
Boil whole Artichokes for 10 minutes, uncovered. Invert to drain and cool.
Gently open center and spread leaves carefully. Scoop out "choke" with sharp spoon, leaving heart.
Melt Butter, add Bread Crumbs, Onions and Cheese. Stuff center of Artichoke and between larger leaves, with mixture and sprinkle generously with more grated Parmesan Cheese.
Bake at 350 degrees for 45 minutes.
Sprinkle with Paprika before serving.

These Artichokes are beautiful and always get raves!

BROILED TOMATOES

4 medium size Fresh Tomatoes
1/4 cup Dry Bread Crumbs
1 cup Parmesan Cheese, grated
1/4 cup Butter, melted

2 tablespoons Shallots, chopped
1 teaspoon Salt
1/8 teaspoon ground Black Pepper

Cut slice from stem end of Tomatoes.
Combine Bread Crumbs, Parmesan Cheese, Butter, Shallots, Salt and Pepper.
Top Tomatoes with this mixture.
Bake in shallow pan at 350 degrees for 30 minutes.
When serving, sprinkle with additional Parmesan Cheese.
Servings: 4.

CHICKEN SALAD

6 Chicken Breasts   1 bunch Celery Hearts, fine-chopped
5 Hard-boiled Eggs, grated   2 cups Boiled Salad Dressing (or Mayonnaise)
1/2 cup Sweet Relish   1/2 cup Water Chestnuts, thin-sliced
8 ounces Stuffed Olives, chopped   Salt and Pepper to taste

Boil Chicken Breasts. Cool, then debone and fine-chop.
Add Eggs, Relish, Olives, Celery and Water Chestnuts.
Blend-in Salad Dressing (Mayonnaise) and add Salt and Pepper; mixing all thoroughly.

FIESTA BRUNCH EGGS

6 Corn Tortillas
1/2 cup Shallots, chopped
1 can (4 ounce size) Green Chiles,
   seeded and chopped
6 ounces White Sauce
1 cup Milk

8 Eggs
3 Tomatoes, peeled and chopped
1 small can Ripe Olives, sliced
2 tablespoons Oil
4 tablespoons Butter
2 cups Cheddar Cheese, shredded

Cut Tortillas into strips.
Mix Onion, Chiles, White Sauce and Milk, then beat-in Eggs.
Place Oil and Half of Butter in electric skillet set at 350 degrees. Add Tortilla strips and fry until crisp.
Reduce heat to 250 degrees, melt remaining Butter and pour-in Egg mixture.
Cook, gently lifting so uncooked Eggs can flow underneath until Eggs are fully set.
Add chopped Tomatoes, drained, sliced Olives and shredded Cheese, to cover Eggs.
Cover pan, turn off heat and allow to stand until the Cheese melts.
Serves 4 to 6.

FETTUCCINE AL FLEMING

1-1/2 cup Butter, melted
2 cups Parmesan Cheese, grated
3/4 cup Whipping Cream

Black Pepper, freshly ground
1 pound Fettuccine, cooked and drained
1 jar (8 ounce size) Beluga Caviar

Place cooked, drained noodles in skillet over low heat.
Add Butter, Cheese, Cream and Caviar. Toss lightly.
Season with freshly ground Black Pepper.
Serves 4 to 6.

GARLIC GREEN BEANS

3 pounds Freshly-picked, tender, young
   Green Beans
2 tablespoons Garlic Salt

1/4 cup Oil
3 tablespoons Lemon Juice
1/4 cup Vinegar

Snap Green Beans. Cook in a small amount of water until just tender, but crisp. Do not overcook!
Mix Garlic Salt, Vinegar, Oil and Lemon Juice with drained Beans.
Chill 6 to 8 hours, stirring occasionally.
Serve cold.

Gayle Barrett, my sister, is a beautiful Southern gal. Most of her meals are traditionally Southern.
She serves these Beans with her Wild Game dinners. You too, will find that they are a delicious
accompaniment to the Game Meats as well as the Game Birds.

JACKSON HOLE JAM AND JELLY

Berry-picking can be an exciting event; and the picking in Jackson is no exception.

During the summer and early fall, one of the main topics of conversation may well be the location of the best berries. Many of the pickers are highly secretive if they find a good spot, as the berries are greatly coveted.

Linda Fleming, the wife of my husband's partner, is a fantastic cook; and she is sharing her special Huckleberry Jam and Chokeberry Jelly recipes with you. She has given me jars of each of them and I can assure you they are both excellent.

WILD HUCKLEBERRY (Vaccinium) JAM

2 quarts Huckleberries   6 cups Sugar
1 package Pectin   Paraffin
Lemon Juice

It takes about 2 quarts of Berries to make 4 cups of fruit.
Wash and crush berries and add 1 cup Water.
Measure 3-3/4 cups Berries and 1/4 cup Lemon Juice. Place in kettle.
Add Pectin to fruit in kettle and stir well.
Over high heat, bring to a boil, stirring constantly to avoid scorching.
Add Sugar, one cup at a time, mixing-in well; and bring to a rolling-boil (a boil that cannot be stirred-down). Boil hard for exactly 4 minutes, then remove from heat.
Skim and ladle into jars.
Use 1 tablespoon melted Paraffin to seal each 6 ounce jar.
Store in a cool place.

Blueberries may be substituted successfully for the Huckleberries.

WILD CHOKECHERRY (Prunus) JELLY

Chokecherries
1/2 cup Lemon Juice
6 cups Sugar

1 package Pectin
Paraffin

Wash and crush ripe fruit.
Add one cup Water and simmer for 15 minutes. Squeeze out juice.
In a large kettle, measure 3 cups of Juice and add 1/2 cup Lemon Juice. Add package of Pectin and stir well.
Place over high heat and bring to a boil, stirring constantly to avoid scorching.
Add Sugar, one cup at a time, to include full amount, mixing-in thoroughly.
Continue stirring and bring to a full rolling boil. Boil hard for exactly 2 minutes.
Remove from heat, skim, and pour into jelly glasses.
Seal well with Paraffin.
Yield: 8 six ounce glasses

JALAPENO JELLY (Less Spicy)

1 cup Green Bell Peppers, ground fine	1-1/2 cups Apple Cider Vinegar
1/4 cup Jalapeno Peppers, groung fine	1 bottle Certo
6 cups Sugar	2 to 3 drops Green Food Coloring

Combine all ingredients in saucepan and bring to a rolling boil.
Boil for 1 minute, then remove from heat.
Cool until tepid. Add bottle of Certo and stir thoroughly, adding food coloring.
Place in jars and seal.

Jalapeno jelly is an outstanding accompaniment for wild game steaks and roasts. A spoonful on the side, tipped onto the meat as it is eaten, lends a spicy flavor which heightens enjoyment of of all lean meats, especially game.

JALAPENO JELLY

3/4 cup Fresh Jalapeno Peppers, seeded
    and ground
3/4 cup Green Bell Peppers, seeded
    and ground

1-1/4 cup White Vinegar
6-1/2 cups Sugar
1 bottle Certo

Combine ground and drained Jalapenos, Bell Peppers, Vinegar and Sugar, and boil for 5 minutes.
Remove from heat and allow to cool for 20 minutes.
Return to heat for 2 minutes, while stirring. Add bottle of Certo and cook for 4 minutes longer.
Pour into jars and cover, or seal with melted paraffin after cooling.

FRESH ASPARAGUS OMELETTE

8 small, Fresh Asparagus Spears
3 tablespoons Butter
2 tablespoons Milk
4 Eggs

1/2 teaspoon Salt
1/8 teaspoon Black Pepper
1/2 cup Swiss Cheese, grated

Cook Fresh Asparagus until tender, then drain. Add Butter and keep warm.
Beat Eggs, Milk and Seasonings with wire whisk.
Cook in Butter in heavy skillet or omelette pan, starting with high heat. As omelette sets, lower heat, loosen edges with spatula and tilt pan to allow uncooked egg mixture to flow underneath. When Eggs are fully set, cover half with the cooked Asparagus, fold over other half and place on serving dish.
Top with grated Swiss Cheese.
Serves 2.

STUFFED MUSHROOMS

1-1/2 pounds large Fresh Mushrooms
1 stick Butter
1/2 cup Bread Crumbs
1/2 cup Green Onion, sliced
8 ounces Fresh or Canned Crab Meat

1/2 cup Fresh Parsley, chopped
1/2 to 1 cup Parmesan Cheese, grated
1/2 pound Velveeta Cheese, grated
Salt and Pepper to taste

Wash Mushrooms and remove stems. Save stems for use in other dishes. Drain Mushroom caps on paper towels.
To prepare stuffing, melt Butter, add Bread Crumbs, Crabmeat, Onion, Parsley and Cheeses.
Stuff Mushroom caps and place in oiled casserole dish. Sprinkle additional Parmesan Cheese on top.
Bake at 325 degrees for 45 minutes, adding additional Parmesan Cheese if desired.
Serves 4 to 6.

SOUTH-OF-THE-BORDER SALAD

1 head Lettuce
4 Fresh Tomatoes, peeled
1/2 cup Shallots, chopped
1/2 cup Cheddar Cheese, grated
6 ounces Corn or Tortilla Chips

1 pound Elk or Deer, ground
1 can (fifteen ounces) Kidney Beans, drained
1 large Avocado
8 ounces Italian Salad Dressing

Toss shredded Lettuce, chopped Tomatoes, Shallots, Cheese and Chips together.
Brown Meat, then mix with Beans and Salt to taste. Simmer 10 minutes.
Add Meat to salad and toss again.
Add sliced Avocado, and add Dressing.
Serves 6.

MEXICAN HOT SAUCE (SALSA CALIENTE)

1 large Fresh Tomato	1 clove Garlic
3 Chile Peppers	2 tablespoons Oil
1 tablespoon Vinegar	Salt and Pepper

Grind together Tomato, Garlic and Chile Peppers. Combine with Oil and Vinegar. Salt and Pepper to taste.

An excellent taste-tingler for use with wild game, or with tostadas or corn chips.

JUDY'S VEGETABLE SALAD

1 cup Safflower Oil
1 cup Sugar
1/2 cup White Vinegar

2 teaspoons Prepared Mustard
1 Garlic Clove (or more) pressed
Salt and Pepper to taste

In the above marinade of combined ingredients, add the following vegetables and hold for 6 to 8 hours, stirring occasionally.

1 can Shoe Peg Corn
1 can Mushroom Pieces
1 can Bean Sprouts
1 can Water Chestnuts, sliced thin
1 large can Pimientos, chopped

1 medium Cauliflower, deleaved and chopped
1 Green Bell Pepper, seeded and chopped
1 small Onion, chopped fine
1 cup Celery, chopped

This unusual salad is wonderful with Barbecue.

FRESH SPINACH SALAD WITH HOT DRESSING

1 pound Fresh Spinach, washed,
  dried and chilled crisp
1/4 cup Oil
2 tablespoons Brown Sugar
1/8 teaspoon Dry Mustard

1/4 cup Green Shallots, sliced
1/4 teaspoon Salt
1-1/2 tablespoons Wine Vinegar
Dash Paprika
1 cup Bacon, crisply fried and crumbled

Snip crisp Spinach into large salad bowl.
Heat oil in skillet and add Brown Sugar, Mustard, Shallots, Salt, Vinegar and Paprika.
Bring to a boil, then remove from heat.
When ready to serve, pour hot dressing over Spinach, coating lightly.
Add crumbled, crisp Bacon and serve immediately.
Serves 4.

RICE PILAF

2 cups Rice
2 Beef Bouillon Cubes
4 cups Water
3 tablespoons Butter

1 Onion, chopped
1/2 teaspoon Salt
2 tablespoons Fresh Parsley, minced
1/2 cup Almonds, slivered and toasted

Boil Rice in Water with added Bouillon Cubes. Cook until tender and all water is absorbed. Saute Onions in Butter, add Salt, Parsley and Nuts. Mix with Rice and fluff.

Because my husband, the hunter, is also a producer of Rice, our family has the privilege of eating Rice every day. We love it! Rice is most versatile, therefore, is not monotonous to serve. Why don't you try some Rice dishes, rather than the traditional potatoes, and see the reaction you get from your family and guests. You will find that I have suggested Rice as the perfect accompaniment to many of the wild game entrees.

VEGETARIAN ENERGY CASSEROLE

3 small Zucchini, diced
1 cup Fresh Mushrooms, sliced
2 tablespoons Soy Oil
3 large Tomatoes, peeled and chopped
3 cups Fresh Spinach, shredded

1 teaspoon Salt
1/2 pound Artichoke Spaghettini or
   regular Spaghetti
8 ounces Swiss Cheese, sliced thin
8 ounces Cheddar Cheese, sliced thin

Saute Zucchini and Mushrooms in Soy Oil until soft.
Add Tomatoes, Spinach, and Salt and simmer 15 minutes.
Cook Spaghettini in large kettle of boiling Salted Water until just tender, about 8 minutes. Drain.
Add to sauce and mix well. Place in casserole dish.
Arrange thin-sliced Cheeses on top and heat under broiler until Cheese in bubbly.
Serves 4.

Highly nutritious.

WILD WEST CASSEROLE

2 cans (4 ounce size) Green Chiles,
  seeded and diced
1 pound Monterrey Jack Cheese, grated
1 pound Cheddar Cheese, grated
4 Eggs

2/3 cup Evaporated Milk
1 tablespoon Flour
1/2 teaspoon Salt
1/8 teaspoon Black Pepper
2 Tomatoes, peeled and sliced

Preheat oven to 325 degrees.
Combine Cheeses and Green Chiles, and place in a 2 quart casserole dish.
Separate Eggs. Beat Whites and set aside.
Combine Egg yolks, Milk, Flour, Salt and Pepper. Mix well until blended fully.
Fold Egg whites into yolk mixture and pour over Cheese mixture in casserole. Use fork to blend through Cheese mixture.
Bake for 30 minutes.
Place Tomato slices on top and bake for an additional 30 minutes.
Serves 4 to 6.

ZUCCHINI CASSEROLE AMANDINE

6 to 8 Zucchini, unpeeled and
    coarsely grated
1 cup Green Onions, sliced
8 ounces Cheddar Cheese, grated

Salt and Pepper to taste
1/3 cup slivered Almonds
Paprika

Boil grated Zucchini and chopped Green Onions in small amount of Water for 5 minutes.
Drain excess Water.
Place in casserole dish and add Salt and Pepper. Sprinkle Cheese and Almonds on top.
Bake only until Cheese melts.
Sprinkle with Paprika to serve.
Serves 4 to 6.

ZUCCHINI VEGETABLE MEDLEY

4 to 6 small, tender Zucchini, sliced
2 Fresh Tomatoes, chopped or
   1 can Tomatoes, drained
1 cup Green Onions, chopped

1 cup Fresh Mushrooms, sliced
1-1/2 cups Cheddar Cheese, grated
Salt and Pepper to taste

Mix Zucchini, Tomatoes, Onions and Mushrooms in a shallow glass casserole dish. Add Salt and Pepper to taste.
Bake at 350 degrees for 20 minutes.
If there is too much liquid, pour off excess.
Top with grated Cheese and bake for 15 minutes more.
Serves 4 or 5.

PRETTY PUMPKIN BREAD

3/4 cup Butter
2-1/2 cups Sugar
4 Eggs
1 can (1 pound size) Pumpkin
2/3 cup Water
3-1/2 cups Unbleached Flour

2 teaspoons Baking Soda
1-1/2 teaspoons Baking Powder
1 teaspoon Salt
1 teaspoon Cinnamon, ground
1 teaspoon Cloves, ground
1/2 cup Pecans or Walnuts, chopped

Cream Butter and Sugar in a large bowl. Add Eggs one at a time, beating thoroughly, then mix in Pumpkin and Water.

In a separate bowl, combine the balance of dry ingredients, mixing thoroughly; then add gradually to the Pumpkin mixture, stirring until the batter is well blended.

Grease and flour baking cans (saved from vegetables, etc., with labels removed and washed clean) so you can make round loaves. Fill 2/3 full with batter and bake at 350 degrees for 35 to 45 minutes, depending upon diameter of the cans. When a toothpick inserted in the loaf comes out clean, it is done.

May also be baked in two greased and floured loaf pans. Divide the batter and bake at 350 degrees for 1 hour and 10 minutes. Test with toothpick. Let cool 15 minutes to remove from cans or pans.

The cool round loaves packaged in plastic bags and secured with dried Fall leaves or flowers, make wonderful remembrance surprises for an ill friend, an elderly aunt or to take to your dinner hostess. Let's take time from this hurried, busy world to "smell the roses"!

ZUCCHINI OR CARROT BREAD

2 Eggs
3/4 cup Sugar
1/2 cup Oil
1 cup Zucchini, unpeeled and grated or
    1 cup Carrot, grated
1 teaspoon Vanilla Extract

1-3/4 cups Flour
1/2 teaspoon Salt
1/2 teaspoon Baking Powder
1/2 teaspoon Baking Soda
1/2 teaspoon Cinnamon, ground
1/2 cup Pecans or Walnuts, chopped

In a large bowl, beat Eggs until foamy.
Add Sugar and Oil, then stir-in Zucchini or Carrots and Vanilla Extract.
In a separate bowl, combine Flour, Salt, Baking Powder, Baking Soda, and Cinnamon.
Add to Zucchini or Carrot mixture and stir-in until well-blended. Add Nuts.
Place in a greased and Floured 9 by 5 by 3 inch loaf pan and bake at 350 degrees for 1 hour 10 minutes, or until done.

I usually make one loaf of Zucchini Bread and one loaf of Carrot Bread at the same time. This way, you have two loaves and only one mess!
Children really love it. It tastes like cake, but is highly nutritious. In fact, this is the only way I can get my boys to eat Zucchini!

POTICA (Yugoslavian Nut Roll)

1/2 cup Granulated Sugar
1-1/2 tablespoons Honey
1 teaspoon Salt
1/4 cup Butter, melted
1 cup Hot Milk
2 packages Active Dry Yeast
1/4 cup Warm Water (110 degrees)
2 Eggs
4-1/2 cups unsifted all-purpose Flour

Filling:
3 Eggs, slightly beaten
4 cups (1 pound) Walnuts, chopped
3 ounces Pecans, chopped
1 cup Brown Sugar, packed
1/3 cup Butter, melted
1-1/2 teaspoons Cinnamon, ground
1 teaspoon Vanilla Extract
2 tablespoons Butter, melted

Heat 1 cup Milk and stir-in Sugar, Salt, Butter and Honey. Let cool to room temperature.
In large bowl, sprinkle 2 packages Yeast over 1 cup Water heated to exactly 110 degrees.
Stir to dissolve Yeast; then stir-in lukewarm Milk mixture.
Add Eggs and 2-1/2 cups Flour. Beat at high speed with electric mixer for 2 minutes. With wooden
spoon, beat-in remaining 2 cups Flour. For proper consistency, 1/2 cup more Flour may be needed.
Knead dough with hands until dough leaves sides of bowl. Place dough in large, lightly-greased bowl
and turn to leave greased side up. Cover with towel and let rise in warm place to double in bulk.
For Filling, combine chopped Nuts, Eggs, Brown Sugar, Honey, 1/3 cup Butter, Cinnamon and
Vanilla Extract. Stir to blend well. Hold to fill loaves for baking.
Punch down dough. On slightly floured board, turn out dough and cover with bowl for 10 minutes.
Roll out dough in rectangle 20 by 30 inches and spread Filling to within 1/4 inch from edge. *

POTICA – Continued

Roll tightly from wide side and pinch edges with fingers to seal. Continue rolling to make uniform in size for full length of roll. Form into coil and place seam side down, on large, greased baking sheet. Cover with towel and allow to rise again, in warm place, until bulk doubles; about 1 hour. Brush-on 2 tablespoons melted Butter and bake in preheated oven, at 350 degrees for 35 to 40 minutes, or until golden brown. This produces a 4 pound loaf. *
    * Dough may be divided and rolled into 2 smaller loaves for filling and baking.

   Sparky Imeson is not only a Super Pilot, but is a multi-talented person as well! He just happens to bake the best bread I have ever tasted; and this is the recipe.
   I have included it, as it is most unusual. In fact, I have never seen it in a cookbook.
   Sparky got the original recipe from his mother, Jane, and has adapted it with the addition of some ingredients and method of preparation. Inclusion of Honey in the dough gives a distinctive flavor. I might add that the bread is quite time-consuming to prepare, but the results are fantastic!

Yum!

SOURDOUGH STARTER

2 cups Flour
2 cups Water, lukewarm

1 Yeast Cake, or
1 package Dry Yeast

Mix ingredients thoroughly in a 2 quart container of crockery, glass or plastic. Do not use metal!
Cover with a double thickness of cheesecloth, and store in a warm place until the "sponge" begins
to bubble, rises and falls back; about 8 to 10 hours.
Stir with a rubber spatula, and let the mixture bubble for about 2 days. The "sponge" must "work"
to achieve a thick texture and a fresh, sour aroma.
After 2 days, stir again with a rubber spatula, place a lid over the cheesecloth and store in the
refrigerator. Label the container.

To replenish Starter: Each time the Starter is used, add equal amounts of warm Water and Flour.
Cover with cheesecloth and allow to bubble overnight, or for 6 to 8 hours, at least.
Replace lid and store in refrigerator.

Did you know that the use of Sourdough has been in existence for 6,000 years?

SOURDOUGH BREAD

4 cups Flour
2 tablespoons Sugar
1 teaspoon Salt

2 tablespoons Melted Shortening or Oil
2 cups Prepared Sourdough Starter

Mix together the Flour, Sugar and Salt. Make a well in the center and pour in the Shortening or Oil.
Add 2 cups of the Prepared Sourdough Starter and blend well with the Flour mixture.
Dough should be soft. If not, add Flour or Liquid (Water or Milk), as required.
Knead for 3 to 4 minutes on cleaned, floured surface.
Cut off chunks of dough to fit pans and set in a warm place to rise.
When doubled in bulk, bake for 50 to 60 minutes in moderate oven.
Test with a straw or toothpick.

BEGUILING BEVERAGES

"Beautiful beverage ideas to accompany your wild game dinners or parties."

CHAMPAGNE TONY

French Champagne   Fresh Strawberries

Fill Champagne glasses with an excellent French Champagne.
Add a large, fresh Strawberry to each.

Beautiful! Elegant! Delicious!

I named this one for an outstanding and famous restaurant in Houston, Texas;
Tony's Restaurant.

FESTIVE PARTY PUNCH

1 can (46 ounce size) Pineapple Juice
1 can (6 ounce size) Frozen Lemonade

1 can (6 ounce size) Frozen Orange Juice
1 bottle (28 ounce size) Ginger Ale*

Mix Pineapple Juice, thawed, but undiluted Frozen Lemonade concentrate and Orange Juice
concentrate, followed by Ginger Ale*.
Add Ice to chill mixture, and for dilution.
Garnish with fresh Orange and Lemon slices and with fresh Strawberries.

A colorful and zesty party beverage.

* Instead of using Ginger Ale, you may substitute either 1 bottle of Champagne or of Light Rum.

HOT WINE

1/2 Lemon, sliced
24 Whole Cloves
2 Cinnamon Sticks
1 cup Sugar

1/2 cup Water
3 cups canned, unsweetened Orange Juice
3 cups canned, unsweetened Pineapple Juice
4 or 5 cups Burgundy Wine

Boil Lemon, Cloves, Cinnamon Sticks, Sugar and Water for 5 minutes. Cool and strain.
Add Orange Juice, Pineapple Juice and Burgundy Wine.
Heat for serving in mugs or heavy, stemmed wine glasses.

Most invigorating on cold winter days!

INDIAN SUMMER SIPPER

Mix equal parts of Dry Red Wine and Fresh Orange Juice. Serve over Ice.

MIMOSAS

1 bottle Champagne   24 ounces freshly squeezed Orange Juice

Mix in equal parts and serve ice cold in stemmed glasses.
For added excitement, add a fresh Strawberry.

Great for brunch, or just anytime!

ISLAND PUNCH

1/2 jigger Pineapple Juice
1 jigger Lemon-Lime Juice
1 jigger Grenadine Syrup

1 jigger Apricot Liquer
4 jiggers Light Rum
Crushed Ice

Fill blender with Crushed Ice and add all other ingredients.
Blend at high speed to smooth consistency. Don't overdo it, and melt the Ice.

Truly refreshing!

JACKSON HOLE SURPRISE

4 ounces Orange Juice,
   freshly squeezed

4 ounces 7-Up
2 tablespoons Grenadine Syrup

Pour into glass, fill with Ice Cubes and stir

A refreshing non-alcoholic drink; or super with Vodka.

JACKSON HOLE SUNRISE

Puree a peeled and cored Fresh Pineapple and its juices in a blender.
Combine with a cold bottle of Dry Champagne in a chilled pitcher.
If Fresh Pineapple is not available, substitute 24 ounces of canned Pineapple Juice.

JACKSON HOLE SUNSET

1 can (46 ounce size) Hawaiian Punch
2 quarts Ginger Ale or 2 bottles Champagne

1 can (6 ounce size) Frozen Orange Juice
1 can (6 ounce size) Frozen Lemonade

Mix Hawaiian Punch, Ginger Ale or Champagne, and thawed, but undiluted Frozen Orange Juice and Lemonade Concentrate together in a punch bowl.
Add block of Ice and garnish with slices of Fresh Oranges and Lemons.
Serves 30 to 36.

RENDEZVOUS PEAK CAVE-IN

1 bottle Red Bordeaux Wine
3/4 cup Sugar

1 small stick Cinnamon
3 Whole Cloves

Mix all ingredients in saucepan and heat to just below boiling-point. Strain.
Add paper-thin slices of Fresh Lemon and serve at once in earthenware mugs.

Sip slowly by the fireside on cold, wintry nights.

ROSE LEMONADE

2 bottles Rose Wine
2 cans (6 ounce size) Frozen Lemonade

1 quart Sparkling Water

Mix together the Rose Wine, Frozen Lemonade Concentrate, undiluted, and Sparkling Water.
Chill and serve.

Most refreshing!

SNOW KING STRAWBERRY BOWL

1 pint box Fresh Strawberries
1/2 cup Powdered Sugar

3/4 cup Sherry Wine
2 bottles Rhine Wine

Rinse and stem strawberries.
Combine Berries, Sugar and Sherry Wine; and allow to stand for several hours.
Pour Rhine Wine and Berry mixture over a block of Ice in the punch bowl.
When chilled, serve in wine goblets.

Truly unusual!

YUMMY DESSERTS

"The finale to a perfect evening is a spectacular dessert. It need not be so "gooey" and calorie-laden that you feel absolutely sinful to eat it. I have some selections for you from the elaborate to the simple-but-beautiful. What a way to end the affair!"

APPLE BLOSSOM CAKE

1 cup Oil
2-1/4 cups Sugar
3 Eggs
1 teaspoon Vanilla Extract
3 cups Flour
1-1/2 teaspoon Baking Soda

1 teaspoon Salt
1 teaspoon Cinnamon, ground
1 teaspoon Nutmeg, ground
1/2 teaspoon Cloves, ground
1 cup Pecans, chopped
3 cups raw Apples, cored and chopped with peels

Cream together Oil, Sugar, Eggs and Vanilla Extract. Add Flour, Baking Soda, Salt, Cinnamon, Nutmeg, Cloves, and Pecans.
Add Apples. Batter will be quite stiff.
Bake in a greased and Floured tube pan at 350 degrees for 1 hour 20 minutes.
Let cool in pan.
Also freezes well.

FABULOUS BAKED BANANAS

8 selected Bananas
2 Eggs
Flour
1 cup Brown Sugar

1/4 to 1/2 pound Butter
1 cup Port Wine
2 Lemons, juiced

Remove skins from 8 firm Bananas. The "pink" ones are best for this purpose.
Dip Bananas into 2 well-beaten Eggs, roll in Flour and place in baking dish.
Cover with 1 cup Brown Sugar and dot with 1/4 to 1/2 pound of Butter.
Pour over this, 1 cup Port Wine and the Juice of 2 Lemons.
Bake uncovered at 325 to 350 degrees for 1 hour.

My mother-in-law, Mrs. Lane Barbour, is the epitome of the Southern Belle. She is truly elegant and loves beautiful things. When you are invited to the Barbour's home for dinner, it is always festive and tastefully done. This is one of her specialties.

YUMMY BROWNIES

1-1/2 sticks Butter
1-1/2 cups Sugar
3 Eggs
1 cup Flour
1/4 cup Cocoa
1/8 teaspoon Salt
1 teaspoon Vanilla Extract
3/4 cup Pecans, chopped

Icing:
1/2 stick Butter
2 tablespoons Cocoa
2 tablespoons Milk
1-1/4 cups Confectioner's Sugar
1/4 cups Pecans, chopped

Preheat oven to 350 degrees. Grease 9 by 9 inch square baking pan.
Cream Butter and Sugar, beating until fluffy; then beat-in Eggs, one at a time.
Add Flour, Cocoa and Salt to mixture, blending well. Stir-in Vanilla Extract and Pecans.
Pour into greased pan and bake for 35 minutes, or until a test toothpick comes out clean
when inserted near the center.

Make Icing while Brownies are baking.
In a saucepan over low heat, melt Butter and stir-in Cocoa and Milk.
Remove from heat and beat-in Confectioner's Sugar and Pecans.
Spread Icing evenly over warm Brownies when done. Cool and cut into squares.

BACK-PACK ENERGY SNACK

1/2 pound Butter, softened
2 cups Brown Sugar
2 Eggs
2 teaspoons Orange or Lemon Rind, grated
3 tablespoons Fresh Orange or Lemon Juice
2 cups Flour

3/4 teaspoon Salt
1 teaspoon Baking Soda
2-1/2 cups Rolled Oats, dry
1/2 cup Coconut, shredded
1-1/2 cups Dried Dates, chopped
1 cup unsalted Mixed Nuts, chopped fine

Cream together softened Butter and Brown Sugar.
Blend-in Eggs, Orange or Lemon Rind and Juice.
In another bowl, combine Flour, Salt, Baking Soda, Oats and Coconut. Stir into creamed mixture and mix thoroughly. Then, blend-in Dates and Nuts.
Drop by tablespoonfuls on ungreased cookie sheets.
Bake at 350 degrees for 15 to 18 minutes, until edges are lightly browned.
Cool on racks.
Store in airtight containers.

ESPRESSO ICE

3 tablespoons Instant Espresso Coffee   4 Ice Cubes
2/3 cup Sugar   Whipped Cream

In a 2 quart saucepan, boil 1 cup Water, and add Instant Espresso Coffee and Sugar, stirring constantly. Reduce heat and simmer 5 minutes, then remove from heat.
Add 1 cup Water and 4 Ice Cubes, stirring until Ice is melted. Pour into refrigerator tray and freeze until firm about 1 inch from edge, about 1 hour and 45 minutes.
Empty into large bowl and beat with electric mixer at medium speed, until smooth and no ice crystals remain.
Divide into 2 refrigerator trays and refreeze for about 1 hour; until nearly solid.
To serve, stir and spoon into parfait glasses. Top with Whipped Cream and serve immediately.
Serves 4.

An unusual dessert treat.

MANGY MOUSSE

8 Eggs
1 package (12 ounces) Semi-Sweet
   Chocolate Chips
1-1/3 sticks Butter

1/4 cup Cognac
1 bar (4 ounce size) Milk Chocolate
3/4 cup Whipping Cream

Separate Eggs. Allow whites to warm to room temperature.
Melt Semi-Sweet Chocolate Chips and Butter in top of double-boiler, stirring constantly.
Remove from heat and add Egg Yolks one at a time, beating well into Chocolate.
Cool for 10 minutes, then add Cognac.
Beat Egg Whites until stiff.
Fold Chocolate mixture into Egg Whites and place in a 1 quart silver bowl. Refrigerate.
Before serving mousse, whip Cream until stiff and place it in a pastry bag.
Squeeze out rosettes to decorate the top of Mousse and add Chocolate curls made from the
Chocolate Bar, formed with a carrot peeler.
Refrigerate until serving time.
Serves 8 to 10.

Elegant and delicious!

HIGH COUNTRY PEANUT BUTTER COOKIES

1-1/2 cups Flour
1/2 cup Sugar
1/2 teaspoon Baking Soda
1/4 teaspoon Salt

1/2 cup Vegetable Shortening
1/2 cup Creamy Peanut Butter
1/4 cup Light Karo Syrup
1 tablespoon Milk

Combine Flour, Sugar, Baking Soda and Salt. Blend-in Shortening and Peanut Butter until mixture resembles coarse meal. Then blend-in Syrup and Milk.
Shape into 2 inch rolls and chill.
Slice 1/8 to 1/4 inch thick and place half the slices on an ungreased cookie sheet.
Spread each slice with 1/2 teaspoon Creamy Peanut Butter, and cover with remaining slices.
Seal edges with a fork.
Bake at 350 degrees for 12 minutes or until browned.
Yield: 2 dozen.

SOUTHERN PECAN PIE

1 cup Light Karo Syrup
3 Eggs, slightly beaten
1/8 teaspoon Salt
1 teaspoon Vanilla Extract

1 cup Sugar
2 tablespoons Corn Oil
1 cup Pecan Halves
1 unbaked Pie Shell, 9 inch size

Combine Karo Syrup, Eggs, Salt, Vanilla Extract and Oil, adding Pecan halves last.
Pour mixture into unbaked Pie Shell.
Bake at 400 degrees for 15 minutes, then reduce heat to 350 degrees and bake 30 to 35 minutes longer.
When pie is done, edges should be set with slightly soft center.

Since I am a native Texan, transplanted to Wyoming part time, I just had to include this recipe for Pecan Pie, as it is one of my favorites.

ON-THE-TRAIL COOKIES

6 cups Flour
1 teaspoon Baking Powder
1 pound Brown Sugar, light
1 pound Butter.

1 cup Pecans, chopped
1 Egg, slightly beaten
1 teaspoon Vanilla Extract

Soften Butter and cream-in Brown Sugar. Add Flour, Baking Powder, Egg, and Vanilla Extract, smoothly blending all together. Add chopped Pecans, distributing evenly throughout the dough. Shape into rolls and chill.
Slice and bake at 350 degrees for about 12 minutes, or until evenly browned.
Yield: 10 to 12 dozen.

SENSATIONAL SUGAR COOKIES

1 cup Butter, room temperature
2/3 cup Sugar
3 Egg Yolks, slightly beaten

1 teaspoon Vanilla Extract
2-1/4 cups Flour

Cream Butter and Sugar together, thoroughly.
Add Egg Yolks one at a time, beating-in to blend; then add Vanilla Extract.
Gradually add Flour until completely smooth throughout the mix. Chill the finished dough.
Roll out on Floured waxed paper and cut into pretty shapes with assorted cookie-cutters.
Bake in preheated oven at 350 degrees for about 12 minutes. Do not let then get too brown.
Remove immediately to paper towels to cool.
Yield: 4 to 5 dozen.

May be topped with an icing of Confectioner's Sugar and Milk mixed to spreading consistency and tinted with food colorings. Sprinkle with colored Sugar.

Beautiful cookies!

SUPER SAND TARTS

6 tablespoons Butter
3 tablespoons Confectioner's Sugar
1 cup Flour

1/2 teaspoon Ice Water
1/2 teaspoon Vanilla Extract
1/2 cup Pecans, chopped fine

Cream Sugar into softened Butter, then add Flour and Pecans. Add Water and Vanilla Extract.
Mixture should be consistency of pie dough. Chill.
Roll small balls of dough between hands and form into crescent shapes to bake.
Bake on ungreased cookie sheet at 350 degrees for 15 to 20 minutes. Do not allow to brown.
While warm, coat with Confectioner's Sugar and allow to cool.
Yield: 1-1/2 dozen.

Recipe may be doubled or tripled successfully.

SNOW KING TREAT

1-1/2 cups Semi-Sweet Chocolate Chips
1/3 cup Butter
1/2 cup Walnuts, chopped fine

1/3 cupGreen Creme de Menthe
1/2 gallon Vanilla Ice Cream

Melt Chocolate Chips and Butter together in top of double-boiler over simmering water, stirring continuously. Remove from heat and stir-in chopped Walnuts.
Line 8 muffin pan cups with souffle cups. Using narrow spatula, spread layer of Chocolate mixture over bottom and sides of paper cups. Place in freezer to harden quickly.
Remove paper liners from Chocolate "cups" before filling to serve.
For filling, add Creme de Menthe to softened Vanilla Ice Cream, whip together and refreeze.
Fill Chocolate cups with the Ice Cream and top with Chocolate shavings.
Return to freezer until time to serve.
Serves 8.

STRAWBERRIES ROMANOFF

1 quart French Vanilla Ice Cream
1 pint Fresh Strawberries, washed and stemmed

1/4 cup Cointreau or Triple Sec

Allow ice cream to soften.
In a bowl, blend-in Liquer and Fresh Strawberries.
Scoop into serving dishes and return to freezer to harden.
When serving, garnish each with a fresh, whole Strawberry.
Serves 6.

ELEGANT ELK - DELICIOUS DEER

INDEX

IMAGINATIVE HAPPENINGS

APPEALING APPETIZERS

ELEGANT ELK - DELICIOUS DEER

UNUSUAL ACCOMPANIMENTS

BEGUILING BEVERAGES

YUMMY DESSERTS

NOTES: